I0479274

# Monetary Anarchy

## *The Separation of Money and State*

Alexander Johann Eser

@alexjeser
monetaryanarchy.com

Copyright © 2023 by Alexander Johann Eser
(@alexjeser | monetaryanarchy.com)
1st edition, April 2023

All rights reserved.

No part of this book may be reproduced, stored in a retrieval system, or transmitted in any form or by any means, electronic, mechanical, photocopying, recording, or otherwise, without the prior written permission of the publisher.

ISBN: 9798389960206

Layout: Pavel Stanishev

**Disclaimer:**

The information provided in this book is for informational purposes only and is not intended to be a source of advice with respect to the material presented. The information and/or documents contained in this book do not constitute legal or financial advice and should never be used without first consulting with a financial professional to determine what may be best for your individual needs.

The publisher and author does not make any guarantee or other promise as to any results that may be obtained from using the content of this book. You should never make any investment decision without first consulting with your own financial advisor and conducting your own research and due diligence. To the maximum extent permitted by law, the publisher and author disclaims any and all liability in the event any information, commentary, analysis, opinions, advice and/or recommendations contained in this book prove to be inaccurate, incomplete or unreliable, or result in any investment or other losses.

Content contained or made available through this book is not intended to and does not constitute legal advice or investment advice and no attorney-client relationship is formed. The publisher and author is providing this book and its contents on an "as is" basis. Your use of the information in this book is at your own risk.

*Dedicated to those who pursue truth, regardless of the consequences,*
*and who are unafraid of what they might find*

# Contents

# Preface

Occasionally in life, we may find ourselves compelled to undertake tasks that aren't necessarily our top preference, but we recognize that if we abstain from them, no one else will, leaving the world in a worse state. Such is my feeling about this book. My desire to impart knowledge about the prospect of monetary anarchism - the separation of money from government authority - and its benefits for humanity stems more from a moral responsibility than a bid to present myself as an economic authority. Moreover our education system has difficulty embracing ideas that defy traditional thinking and reach beyond specific disciplines. If your work deviates from the consensus, it will not be recognized with citations. Lacking citations, your reputation within academics will not progress, and subsequently, you will be unable to obtain a high-ranking role within academic institutions. This, in consequence, impacts your financial security as you struggle to find employment in the academic field. As such, numerous academics feel forced to endorse mainstream beliefs for the sake of self-preservation, without considering the motivations they are promoting.

Is there any book, article, or publication that promotes the separation of money creation from government control, advocates for society's adoption of decentralized currency, and bears "anarchy" in its title that appears to be mainstream economics? Certainly not. That's the reason this book exists, authored by a tech entrepreneur with no ambitions of being the next confused economist. Instead, my goal is to appeal to discerning, logical, and fundamental thinkers who are unencumbered by intellectual dishonesty in order to protect their careers. In the spirit of Picasso, I must admit that I embrace the idea that good artists copy while great artists steal. Accordingly, throughout the text, you may encounter some of my own unique ideas mixed with those of prominent libertarians like Ludwig von Mises, Murray Rothbard, Hans-Hermann Hoppe, David Friedman, and Jörg Guido Hülsmann (among others). Also it is essential to recognize the influence of Nassim Nicholas Taleb's work on my thinking, and in his honor, I must acknowledge my unwillingness to adhere to academic standards or provide proper attribution. When unsure, presume that my points are not original. Additionally, I will torment the minds of experts by oversimplifying complex subjects without elaboration, trusting readers to research arguments that challenge their reasoning. It is far more crucial for me to stimulate the thoughts of curious readers rather than conform to any academic norms.

As for the MBA business professionals who wish to impress their coworkers or peers, the TL;DR version of the book is quite straightforward. So, even if you don't read the entire book, please do one favor for humanity: spread the word!

**TL;DR:** Money serves as the lifeblood of society, transmitting essential information about the scarcity of goods through the market mechanism. However, active interference in the money market by nation-states distorts price signals, resulting in a massive misallocation of resources and giving an unfair advantage to a select group of political insiders at the expense of society. This scheme is enforced by the state apparatus through its monopoly on violence, as it feeds on its subjects like a parasite without consent. States impose a regime of economic terror on humanity through taxation and the unethical act of inflation, exerting their monopoly on money production. The separation of money production from the state offers humanity the opportunity to restore virtue, promote peace, and advance humanitarian progress. For the first time in history, these possibilities have become achievable through the emergence of the trustless Bitcoin network and the implications illuminated by its technical features.

# Introduction

There is a growing unease in our world, a sense that something is not quite right. It is hard to pinpoint the exact source of this feeling, as it manifests in various ways: the gradual erosion of family values, increasing social inequalities, the disappearing middle class, and the need for multiple jobs to provide for one's family. Furthermore mental health struggles and depression are common, quality time with loved ones is scarce, young people grapple with understanding their roles in society, and access to housing, healthcare, and education feels more and more like a privilege. The concept of a fulfilling life feels like a relic of the past, replaced by a dehumanizing present that treats us as cogs in a machine. This societal imbalance causes distress for many, leading to a rise in extreme viewpoints on both ends of the political spectrum. People search for easy answers, dividing themselves into allies and adversaries - surely, there must be someone to blame for our troubles, right? Unfortunately, pointing fingers at those we disagree with won't solve our problems. Rather than resorting to blame, we should collectively reflect on why our world looks the way it does, and explore the potential steps we can take to change our course. But for many, this task may seem overwhelming. Where should one start? Which questions should be asked? Whose information can be trusted? The subsequent book embodies the zenith of my personal quest to understand the world.

The spark that inspired me to reflect on the current state of our society was my initial encounter with Bitcoin. I dismissed it at first, assuming it was just another get-rich-quick scam and a tool for criminals. As it turns out, I couldn't have been more wrong. In my opinion, Bitcoin holds the keys to solving the vast majority of humanity's challenges. While this might seem like an outlandish claim, it's important to consider that those who have dedicated a significant amount of time (about 1,000 hours or more) to studying Bitcoin often arrive at the same conclusion. Fundamentally, Bitcoin offers a means of organizing ourselves as a society that is free from corruption, coercion, and centralization. It ensures that everyone plays by the same rules and that these rules cannot be manipulated for personal gain. Adopting this fair coordination method would allow our civilization to reach new heights by negating the need to grapple with the consequences of our existing, compromised system. To achieve this, it is crucial for us to acknowledge the flaws in our current way of organizing society and to actively work towards rectifying the challenges we face. How can we ensure a fair, violence-free system that provides a strong economic foundation for our collective future? Although addressing our societal problems may be challenging, and these may not be the thoughts that preoccupy most people on a typical Saturday afternoon, it is crucial that we dedicate time to examining our current social condition instead of blindly conforming to established norms.

When discussing "coordination mechanisms" or "societal organization," what I am essentially referring to is "money." Money is the cornerstone of every society, permeating every aspect of our lives. It functions as information, language, expression, power, representation of time, and most importantly, a human invention. What is unnatural is the use of money as a tool for widespread devastation through the manipulation of our financial institutions and the economic oppression of a large segment of the population by monetizing debt. This is orchestrated by political elites under the guise of statism, allegedly for societal improvement. To break this cycle, we should adopt the Bitcoin network as our preferred means of separating government from monetary creation, much like political authority was once detached from religious institutions through statism centuries ago.

The outcome of this separation is monetary anarchy, which, on the surface, might seem like a contemporary spin on the French Revolution that leads to bloodshed on Wall Street. However, the truth is quite contrary. While the word "anarchy" often carries negative connotations, it doesn't have to. Anarchy essentially means the absence of governance or leadership, which in turn implies the absence of manipulation, corruption, and coercion. In an unregulated and interference-free market, all participants engage anarchically. For example, consider dating: No one can dictate the rules governing relationships. Jane has sovereignty over her own body, and John has no control over it without violating her individual property rights to herself. If the dating market were anything other than completely anarchic, society will strongly protest.

Dating benefits from being easily perceived as a market that must be free from external influence and can only function morally in a state of anarchy. Money, on the other hand, is much more complex for most people, making it difficult to grasp why monetary anarchy benefits society as a whole. So, even if you find it challenging to keep up with subsequent chapters, remember that adopting monetary anarchy is the only intellectually defensible moral stance we can take to create a better future, much like the only morally defensible position for the dating market is the anarchy of choice (the "why" will be addressed later).

To clarify and comprehend the advantages of monetary anarchy, we will first explore the origin of money production, then examine the emergence of money monopolies under the pretense of statism and the reduction of individual freedoms. Following that, I will discuss the evolution of states from aristocracy to monarchy to democracy and why they are neither necessary nor morally justifiable. Next, I will propose an alternative system, specifically anarcho-capitalism, and ultimately envision a new era for humanity, one that is liberated from the shackles of economic apprehension and powered by a decentralized monetary framework. However, before delving into a discussion about society as a whole, we must first address another topic: How do we determine our knowledge?

# The Origin of Knowledge

Examining the origins of knowledge acquisition may seem like an unusual starting point when considering a society built on monetary anarchy. However, it is crucial for our deliberations to comprehend where definitive knowledge originates and whether there is even such a thing as definite knowledge. Why? Because all arguments we present to persuade others of our viewpoint will inevitably lead to discussions about how we know that our approach is accurate. Unsurprisingly, we have to go against mainstream thinking on this matter. Science labels all knowledge that is not derived from observable experiments as "pseudoscience." We are taught in academic institutions that we need to run statistical tests and crunch numbers to definitively prove something as true or false. This methodology, known as "empiricism," is the prevalent approach for being regarded seriously within academia. According to our educational system, this suggests that all knowledge stems from experience and cannot be obtained in any other manner, barring a few exceptions. However, is this entirely accurate? Gaining knowledge through experience implies that if something cannot be observed, it must be untrue or insignificant. For instance, one might contend that because of Bitcoin's significant price fluctuations, it cannot function as a currency. Is this evaluation precise, or does a parallel universe exist alongside ours where Bitcoin is the primary means of monetary exchange?

To resolve this conflict, let's examine the mathematical equation "2+2=5." Remarkably, this simple statement has the ability to disturb our rational minds. What could be the reason? It's because we've learned that 2+2=4, and if we went around claiming that 2+2 amounts to 5, we might find ourselves in a psychiatric facility. However, imagine if we altered all calculators in New York City so that they display the sum of 2+2 as 5 rather than 4. We would still feel uncomfortable and recognize that something is not right. Why is that? We have just witnessed the observed reality that 2+2=5, not 4, as demonstrated by the significant statistical evidence from thousands of calculators. Surely, this must be accurate?

It turns out, it's not. Mathematical principles are universal and not limited by location. Identical reasoning is valid in various places and times. Even a child who is homeschooled and taught by their parents that 2 plus 2 equals 5 would soon discover that this is false. The only factor capable of altering math is perception. Two plus two can indeed equal two, rather than four.

How is this possible? Through the modification of inputs: observing two lions plus two gazelles yields four animals in total, yet there remain only two lions.

In essence, mathematics demonstrates a fundamental truth that all entities must comply with. The understanding of mathematics (distinct from the knowledge produced by mathematics) is referred to as "a priori knowledge." This knowledge is acquired without relation to reality. Even in the absence of the surrounding world, mathematics and logic remain valid. The phrases "a priori" and "a posteriori" primarily serve to indicate the basis for acquiring certain knowledge. A specific proposition is considered "a priori" if it can be understood without relying on any experience except for the process of learning the language in which the proposition is conveyed. Conversely, a proposition that is "a posteriori" is learned through experience, or as mentioned earlier, via empiricism.

To put it in simpler terms, there exist two realities: one that we recognize as truth by definition or logic, and another that we discern as truth through observation. Embracing this differentiation is vital for comprehending the arguments that I will introduce later on. To emphasize this concept, here are a few examples:

| A priori: knowledge through logic | A posteriori: knowledge through observation |
|---|---|
| My father's brother is my uncle. | My father's brother has black hair. |
| Blue is a color. | The ocean is blue. |
| 2 + 2 = 4. | 2 quarts of any liquid added to 2 more quarts of any liquid = 4 quarts of liquid. |
| All bachelors are unmarried males. | All bachelors in the U.S. are taxed at a different rate from married men. |
| Happiness is an intrinsic good. | Happiness is the result of doing what you like. |

Instead of just accepting the statement that John is the uncle of his brother's son, we can use logical reasoning to verify its accuracy. However, we cannot simply assume that John has black hair as a fact, as he can also have brown or blonde hair. To verify his hair color, we must observe it. Additionally, the idea that blue is not a color is impossible, so we can confirm this without observation. Nonetheless, it is not guaranteed that all oceans are blue. So where does definite knowledge come from?

Common sense suggests that it is likely that neither methodology is entirely accurate. Some knowledge cannot be obtained through logic alone, and not all knowledge arises from empiricism (observation). Nonetheless, as previously discussed, certain aspects of knowledge can unquestionably be deemed accurate via either of the two methods. The disagreement between rationalism (understanding through reasoning) and empiricism (comprehension via observation) has its origins in the time of ancient Greek thinkers and features prominent advocates for both viewpoints.

Immanuel Kant was the pioneering philosopher who sought to reconcile these methodologies. He introduced the concept of "transcendental idealism" as his solution to the problem. This seemingly complex idea can be rephrased as the notion that our minds actively contribute to shaping our experience of the world. According to Kant, we can't know things as they exist independently but can only understand them as they appear to us. Consequently, our perception of the world isn't solely based on external reality but is also affected by our cognitive processes, including concepts, categories, and modes of reasoning. Kant posited that the world we perceive is a blend of sensory information and the mental framework employed to interpret this data. This framework consists of innate, a priori concepts such as space, time, causality, and substance, which are embedded within our mind's structure. These concepts enable us to arrange our experiences into meaningful patterns and comprehend the world around us. Kant contended that empiricists are misguided if they believe empiricism is the only valid method for attaining knowledge because they insist that it's impossible to transcend experience. Rationalists are also mistaken because they claim it's feasible to surpass experience through theoretical reason. For Kant, both approaches were valid and complementary.

Similar to Kant, readers might prefer a balanced stance between these two extremes. Regrettably, mainstream economic theory doesn't share this view and dismisses all knowledge derived from "a priori" reasoning instead of observation. If you feel that no knowledge can emerge from logic concerning economics and monetary theory, then it's time to set this book aside. In the end, all arguments I can present for or against a decentralized monetary system will lead to a debate about the legitimacy of "a priori knowledge" versus "a posteriori knowledge.

However, if you allow logic the opportunity to transform our observed reality, the first task is to identify a theoretical framework for economics. This framework should encompass a series of principles that remain accurate, no matter the reality we perceive, much like mathematical equations. Fortunately, there is a consensus amongst academics regarding the origin of this economic logic; all evidence points to Ludwig von Mises and his economic methodology known as Praxeology. His straightforward yet brilliant idea is that human beings possess limited resources, or "means," but they have infinite wants and desires. In order to fulfill these wants and desires, individuals must make choices about how to use their resources. As long as people have finite resources and infinite desires, they will consistently make choices and take actions to satisfy their needs. This understanding (formally referred to as an axiom) must be accurate because it cannot be disproven without either conceding its truth or engaging in self-contradiction. This is because anyone attempting to refute it would have to utilize limited resources, such as time and mental effort, to do so. This would be classified as an action. As a result, the "action axiom" denier would either contradict themselves or be compelled to acknowledge the legitimacy of the action idea. This implies that economic knowledge can, in fact, be obtained through logic, and we do not need to witness it firsthand to accept it as true.

Reevaluate the earlier statement and ponder on it. Humans have desires and need to act to fulfill those desires. If we want to disprove the statement, we must personally act since we have the desire to refute it. Therefore, we cannot disprove it without creating a contradiction. As a result, we can make assertions about human actions before we even execute them. All human actions combined makeup economics, which means we can make assertions about economics that are accurate ("a priori knowledge") without the requirement to observe them ("empiricism"). We can determine how the world should be instead of how we experience it. We might refer to such a world as utopia because we may never witness it come to fruition, but we can endeavor to progress towards that economic framework to build a more prosperous future. In other words, a set of economic rules based on deductive reasoning enables us to identify facts about our world without needing to prove them right, as they are universally true. The striking difference between these facts and the current state of the world we inhabit may be startling, but that does not render them any less accurate.

Regrettably, state intervention and academic theories have imposed an alternative perspective on society, combining empirical observation and economics in an effort to incorporate data and measurements into monetary theory. As a result, they try to create fixed relations between variables where none exist. This method fails to take into account the subjective nature of value and the complexity of human behavior. For example, they may argue that reducing taxes by a certain percentage will lead to a predictable increase in economic growth, suggesting that this pattern will be consistent across different nations and time periods. However, this argument is flawed since human actions are influenced by individual values and are therefore unique, making it impossible to establish fixed relationships. Economic events are unpredictable and cannot be repeated, unlike controlled scientific experiments.

In reality, the market is a complex mechanism that collects and processes information, generating outcomes based on the data it assesses. Fixed relationships do not exist in this context, and interfering with the market process essentially implies that a small group of decision-makers holds greater knowledge than the cumulative choices made by all market participants. This mindset exemplifies human hubris. Unfortunately, mankind has a penchant for arrogance. We consider ourselves superior to nature (e.g., we have the ability to fly), so what is the harm in assuming we can supersede the inner workings of the market? Yet, we never truly transcend the laws of nature. Airplanes still function under the principles of physics, and any attempt to ignore them leads to disastrous consequences for those who dare. The same cannot be said for the repercussions of ignoring fundamental economic truths derived from logical deduction.

Economists who determine the financial destiny of nations are seldom held responsible for the accuracy of their forecasts. As a result, it is often easier to make a crowd-pleasing decision rather than one that is solidly grounded in reason.

Why do mainstream economists, politicians, and academics seem so quick to dismiss the potential for a priori knowledge about money and economics? To grasp the reasons behind their behavior, we need to scrutinize their individual incentives. This fundamental fact allows us to understand why the field of economics is hesitant to be guided by logic. If a set of infallible rules is derived from logic, there is no room for mistakes. The equation of 2+2 only has one answer. However, the moment empiricism comes into play, countless solutions for any issue arise. If the current outcome of your hypothesis testing does not meet your preferences or comply with your political beliefs, altering the hypothesis or variables becomes easy. In practical terms, this means that governments and their appointed economists can consistently find reasons to interfere in the market process under the façade of economic empiricism. Essentially, governments have developed an excuse to behave as they wish without being constrained by logic.

As a result, our monetary and political systems are founded on deceit. The deception is so widespread that grasping its extent is difficult. Yet, the book presented here aims to achieve precisely that. The following text is an appeal to readers: either become convinced that economic truth based on logic matters or acknowledge that the system we live in and its representatives intentionally disregard economic rationality. With an open mind, common sense, and reasoning, readers are invited to join as I investigate the formation of an alternate monetary reality that allows humanity to thrive.

# The A-B-C of Money

# Natural Money

Previously, I mentioned that money serves as the thread that connects humanity and enables coordination. When our currency becomes distorted, human actions are disrupted and misdirected. Monetary value acts as the beacon around which humans operate. Prices inform us what our fellow humans find valuable and what they do not. Which items should we produce more of, and which ones should we abandon? As such, our journey to comprehend the world begins with an examination of money. What exactly is money, where does it originate, and why does it have value? Why is the state the sole institution authorized to create it?

In seeking answers to these questions, we can alternatively ponder the reverse: What would a world without money look like? In the absence of money, we have to trade or barter items we produce for those we desire. This process introduces a plethora of challenges. First, we face the issue of coincidental encounters or double coincidences, where we must locate someone who wants to exchange their goods simultaneously with our own. This may seem trivial, but what if the items you wish to trade are perishable, such as apples? Another aspect to consider is the problem of measuring value. How many bushels of hay equate to the worth of a cow? How can one trade a portion of a cow for an apple? Extending this idea, we may even question the necessity of trading at all. Why can't everyone be self-reliant and attend to their own needs?

The straightforward response is that productivity increases through the division of labor. People generate a greater output collectively than individually. Even for someone who excels in all tasks, dividing labor is a logical approach. If the market values apples twice as much as bananas and Harry is a more skilled apple and banana farmer than John, should Harry cultivate both fruits? The answer is no. Because Harry possesses a competitive edge in growing the more popular fruit (apples), he should concentrate solely on cultivating apples and exchange them for bananas in the market. By focusing on apple production, he will be better off than if he attempts to grow both fruits. Conversely, John can forgo apple farming and produce something (bananas) the market desires. However, how can Harry and John trade their products if they cannot find anyone willing to exchange their goods at the right time?

A medium of exchange is needed to resolve the situation. To overcome the issues related to direct exchange, everyone must agree on an item that can be universally traded for all other goods through indirect exchange. This universally exchangeable item must possess several qualities to meet the demands of its users. It should be durable, non-perishable, easily transportable, divisible, fungible (i.e., adhere to a uniform standard), and have a limited supply to maintain value due to scarcity. Moreover, it should be effortlessly identifiable and widely accepted by all market participants. In essence, it must be the most marketable commodity - the one that everyone desires. An item that meets these specifications becomes natural money, satisfying the market's need for a store of value, unit of account, and medium of exchange.

Can a new form of money simply be introduced into the market, or does the market need to choose a preferred product to serve as a medium of exchange? To address this question, consider the scenario of providing dollar bills to our prehistoric ancestors. Would they begin exchanging meat and berries for these dollar bills? They would not. For an item to be accepted as money, it must develop organically within the marketplace and possess value beyond its potential monetary worth. Simply put, it is extremely risky for someone to trade their goods for a medium of exchange without knowing if it could be resold in the market. Therefore, the monetary item must be marketable and have inherent value. To prehistoric humans, dollar bills hold no intrinsic worth. Therefore, to become money, everyone must trust that others will accept these dollar bills as a medium of exchange. This suggests that the most marketable commodity is the prime contender among all goods to become money. Being able to consistently trade my goods for this natural money-contender, I can start measuring my items using that currency's unit of account, eventually leading to money as we know it.

Historically, humans have utilized a vast range of commodities as money: cigarettes, shells, gemstones, cattle, cotton, copper, silver, gold, and numerous other items. If communities worldwide can independently choose their preferred currency, various currency options would likely emerge because different commodities best embody the desired attributes of money in different regions. In some areas, gold may not be easily obtainable, leading to a more accessible product taking the role of local currency. This is not to say that gold lacks value in such communities. A free-market system communicates the worth of goods through pricing, which results in the coexistence of multiple currencies within the same society. Copper, silver, and gold would have exchange rates, enabling small transactions with copper, medium ones with silver, and larger ones with gold according to their current market values. The non-coercive monetary selection process, originating from individual choices, enables the most marketable commodity to rise to the top of the money hierarchy. The selection's outcome is a posteriori knowledge, as logically predicting the winner is unfeasible, making money an intrinsically social and human product.

## Credit Money

How is it that we have paper currency today, or arguably not even physical currency, but digital cash? How can something with no inherent value in the market function as money? To better comprehend this occurrence, let's envision a woman named Heidi who wishes to sell a perishable item such as meat to Lisa. She slaughters one of her chickens and sets the meat aside for Lisa to collect. Lisa, who lives a day's journey away from Heidi, realizes upon arriving at Heidi's home that she has forgotten her gold coins. What should Heidi do? Discard the meat reserved for Lisa? Both parties would be worse off. Lisa has expended time and energy in getting to Heidi's house and is famished, while Heidi has already killed one of her chickens and wants compensation. The solution is an IOU (I Owe You) agreement, essentially a piece of paper that Lisa can issue, promising that anyone who redeems the IOU will receive gold coins. She hands the IOU to Heidi. The next time they meet, Heidi will redeem her IOU, and Lisa will pay her in gold coins. In this instance, we refer to credit money, which relies on the crucial assumption that Heidi trusts Lisa to repay her, based on their shared history. If Lisa has a poor reputation for not repaying her IOUs, no market participant will accept an exchange based on credit.

But what if Heidi moves away the following day and never encounters Lisa again? She can attempt to sell the IOU to her neighbor, Harriet. Since Lisa pays anyone who redeems the IOU with gold coins, it holds inherent value, even if the IOU is a mere piece of paper. The critical aspect here is that the piece of paper is supported by gold coins. Therefore, paper and digital currency can only ever possess value if they are supported by something of value in the market. Additionally, as it must be backed, this type of credit money can never be as prevalent as natural money, as its supply (claims on natural money) is constrained by the supply of natural money while also carrying inherent risks. Unlike cash exchange, which is the direct settlement of liabilities between two parties, the redemption of an IOU can only occur later. The holder of the IOU bears the risk of the issuer's bankruptcy, and in case of default, the debt collector is left with nothing. As a result, credit money can only naturally expand if it is supported by natural money, and IOU issuers are credible. We have already determined that money as a commodity in the free market is in constant competition with other commodities, with the most marketable commodity winning the battle for the monetary crown. If unsupported paper currency were to compete in such a market against natural money, it is crowded out.

# Money Production

In practical terms, how does money come into being in a free market environment? Precious metals, particularly gold, evolve as the most marketable commodities that possess all the characteristics required to be deemed exceptional money. To better satisfy these criteria, it is necessary to convert precious metals into coins, enhancing their divisibility and portability. Carrying around large amounts of gold and silver is not feasible for everyday use, and according to the division of labor concept, it is logical that several entrepreneurs join the money production industry to create enough coins for the local economy to operate efficiently. It is likely that those who mint money would not even be responsible for extracting gold from the earth; instead, each stage of the money production value chain is its own business. Similar to how a clothing store has customers, money minters also have clients, adhering to market rules by providing the finest possible products. If consumers were dissatisfied with the product, as might happen if the money minter attempted to defraud them by selling coins at face value but using inferior metals, that specific monetary production entrepreneur will go out of business, with only the most reputable minters remaining in the marketplace.

A potential criticism of this market mechanism is that an economy may require more money to grow than minters can provide. This is indeed true, but as previously mentioned, it is improbable that only one type of coin would serve as currency. If the market demands more gold coins but gold has run out and no new coins can be produced, the value of existing gold coins rises. This, in turn, enhances gold's purchasing power and the exchange rate of gold to silver, subsequently increasing the demand for silver coins to make up for the shortage of gold on the market. If silver is also depleted, demand will transition to copper and so forth. The market then replaces the need for superior money with a slightly lower-quality money that is more readily available while valuing the scarcer currency higher. This substitution of demand continues until the market's needs are met.

Is it not possible for the minters to exploit their unique position in society and produce vast amounts of money for their own gain? As long as minters are honest and do not debase the coins they are selling, the market will keep them in check due to the law of diminishing returns which prevents them from blatantly exploiting their control over the money supply. The law of diminishing returns constrains the production of coins in all free markets, indicating that each subsequent coin produced holds less value for the producer compared to the one before it. In the same way as any other enterprise, money minters must make sensible decisions when dealing with scarce resources. Therefore, they will always allocate their capital to initiatives offering the highest returns. These returns are determined by the individual preferences of all market participants and their needs for various goods. As a result, the creation of money within a free-market society is fully integrated into the division of labor phenomenon and cannot exceed the boundaries established by the market process. The market will consistently stay one step ahead of the money minter, ensuring they are kept in check.

# Inflation

What happens if the money entrepreneurs were not honest though and tried to exploit their clientele by rendering the law of diminishing returns obsolete?

As a money minter motivated by greed, I can either surreptitiously sell my clients debased coins that contain less valuable metal than they assume or I can use my fraudulent coins to directly buy products in the market. In both cases returns on money produced do not diminish and the money supply increases beyond its natural state. In such a scenario we speak of "inflation" or an inflated money supply. Originating from the Latin term "inflare," inflation fundamentally shrinks the savings of individuals possessing currency because when there is more money available in the market, its value decreases assuming the quantity of goods remains consistent.

Accordingly, for a short period at the risk of being exposed, money producers can defraud the market. It is crucial to recognize the dishonest and deceitful intent behind the inflation process. The money producer is well aware of their deeds and plans to sell the produced coins at a higher market value than the precious metal content warrants. Merchants who trade their goods for counterfeit money obtain less value for their products than originally agreed upon. Nefarious minters can take advantage of their clients through inflation, which can readily be identified as morally reprehensible.

However, since coins are sold by weight (which also makes the origin of currency names evident as, for instance, "British Pound"), clients can check the weight of the coins to avoid being duped. Consequently, as soon as the market realizes that there is more money in circulation than expected, prices rise to account for the increased money supply, and the fraudster will go out of business. The corresponding adjustment period is known as the Cantillon effect, during which resources are misallocated, and the market becomes distorted. It should be plainly evident, however, through simple logic, that the money supply must be neutral - meaning that an increase or decrease in the money supply has no real influence on the local economy because prices will adapt as quickly as possible to the new situation. A change in the amount of money available does not imply that our available resources have changed.

If there is ten times more money, everything will merely cost ten times more than it did before, rather than there suddenly being ten times more products available.

Yet, our current economic principles, mainly advocated by John Maynard Keynes and the neoclassical school of economics, assert that the concept of monetary neutrality is flawed, and that fluctuations in the money supply have real, short-term consequences for the economy. This idea supports the belief that we can manipulate the economy at will, with the ability to regulate production and unemployment in the short term. These short-term adjustments are then believed to influence long-term economic prospects. Consequently, the economy can be operated much like a machine at the discretion of the institution controlling the money supply. In the present day, this is a central bank, but in the hypothetical scenario mentioned earlier, it could also be a monopoly held by the money minters. One must wonder how much opium one needs to consume to genuinely believe this to be true. While constructing an economic system that exploits its constituents may be the observable reality we see today, it can never be the fundamental truth of monetary theory.

Let's revisit our narrative about money minters and the reasons why it is challenging to nefariously inflate the supply of commodity money. In a free society with no entry barriers to the money production market, anyone can start issuing their own currency or try counterfeiting a successful minter's coins by using less or no precious metals. However, these counterfeit coins can be easily detected, as most minters engrave distinct patterns. Coins can also be cut or melted to verify their legitimacy. Although minters and counterfeiters can potentially deceive users of commodity money, it remains a challenging endeavor since the value certification is directly stamped onto the precious metal.

However, what happens when the underlying commodity value is removed from the certificate that attests to the value's availability, as in the case of Lisa issuing an IOU to Heidi? Lisa can provide an IOU without possessing the necessary coin to repay Heidi. While such an action may resemble a morally corrupt crime, it becomes more difficult to detect. As a result, identifying fraudulent credit money transactions as inflationary thievery is more complicated.

Taking into account safety and practicality, particularly in the past, carrying large bags of gold and silver coins might not have been the wisest choice for an individual. Usually, when there is discomfort, profit follows. As a result, markets evolve and provide a solution to alleviate this discomfort. Savvy business people can establish money storage facilities and provide custodial services to the market. One can pay a set fee to have their coins safeguarded by the security services of the money storage facility. In return, the businessperson issues a certificate indicating that it can be redeemed for a specific amount of coin. Clients can then trade these certificates amongst themselves, streamlining the market process and further reducing friction in commerce. The exchange of certificates functions as long as everyone involved trusts the money storage facilities to keep their coins secure and not use them for personal benefit. Unfortunately, throughout history, the temptation to misuse the property rights of the rightful coin owners has always been too strong to resist.

Just as coin minters can stamp an incorrect certificate on their coins, money storage facility operators can inflate the money supply by issuing certificates without actually possessing the corresponding precious metals in storage. Alternatively, they can use the valuable metals entrusted to them to make purchases directly in the markets. In either case, the money warehouses lack sufficient precious metal holdings to cover all the liabilities they have towards their clients. As a result, they have not full reserves, but fractional reserves. If all clients decide to redeem their money certificates at the same time, it leads to a situation called a bank run. This means that the facilities where money is stored will not be able to pay back all their clients. It is important to note that money warehouse operators can already run a profitable business by providing security and custody services to the market, but excessive greed turns them into criminals.

It doesn't take long for money warehouse operators to realize that money can generate more money and that they can benefit from participating in the profitable banking industry. They can offer loans and receive interest payments in addition to the principal amount, representing their profit. At its core, this practice is not inherently wrong. Any market participant can lend out their savings as a loan and earn interest. If money storage facility operators lend out their profits earned through their custody service business, there would be no ethical issue at hand. However, banking and lending become an immoral act of theft when money storage facility owners issue loans using their custody service clients' money, which was never theirs to lend, and then profit from the interest payments.

Consider the following scenario: your best friend goes on vacation for a month and entrusts you with the keys to her house so you can care for her plants and ensure everything stays in order. In response, you put her apartment on Airbnb and profit from renting it out. If you rent out your own apartment, there is no ethical issue. However, renting out someone else's property without their consent and profiting from the rental fee is an immoral act of theft.

Financial services can often appear as complex as rocket science, and financial professionals have every incentive to let their business appear complex so the average citizen does not understand what is going on. This is illustrated by the fact that banks, when providing loans using their own funds, should issue individual IOU certificates in addition to certificates representing the commodity money they store for clients. By using identical certificates for both custodial services and loans, the money warehouse banker combines two separate service lines without the consent of their customers. Consequently, market participants need to find a trustworthy money warehouse operator if they want to keep their savings safeguarded from fraud. It is important to note that there is nothing inherently wrong with fractional reserve banking. If the money warehouse operator also wants to function as a banker, they can communicate this to their clientele. They may advertise a 90% reserve ratio, enabling them to lend 10% of their holdings and profit from interest payments. This profit can then be used to reduce custody fees, benefiting both parties. However, experience has shown that banks rarely communicate the nature of their fractional reserve operations to the users who finance the business. From the beginning, bankers are eager to mix certificates and make it difficult for outsiders to understand what is happening, which can lead to confusion and fraudulent practices.

In a twist of irony, the offense of undisclosed fractional reserve banking could have developed as a free-market reaction to another crime. It is evident that a warehouse containing commodity money is a tempting target for unscrupulous individuals looking to obtain a large amount of value with minimal effort. While burglars, raiders, and foreign invaders might come to mind, their impact is negligible compared to the ultimate violator of private property: the state. To fund their war endeavors, kings and governments often turned to banks for support, forcing monetary depositories to find ways to safeguard their client deposits from government reach. Ironically, they accomplished this by loaning out the very funds they were entrusted to hold securely.

Nonetheless, inflation, defined as theft through confusion and intention, can never be viewed as a net gain for humanity in any economic scenario. When the money supply inflates, the value of money diminishes, and its purchasing power decreases. It is akin to money having an expiry date or shelf life. If the money supply inflates, the money you have earned loses its value, and you can no longer purchase as many goods as before. Waiting too long may even render your money worthless. Is it morally justifiable for you to receive currency as compensation for your labor when this currency has an intrinsic shelf life, and you cannot control when you can use it without suffering financial losses? This doesn't seem like a fair deal.

In the 21st century, those who control money production can openly announce a crime on television without any reaction, or worse, convince people that being robbed has a positive aspect. This is a clear indication of how effective those in charge of money production and banking have been at obfuscating their tactics over the centuries. Therefore, it is essential to educate ourselves on these matters and understand how banks and other financial institutions operate to protect our assets and make informed decisions.

# The Monopolization of Money

# Outlawing the Free Money Market

It is clear that in a free market, commodity money can be compromised by dishonest individuals through forgery or acquisition, but this does not mean it can be entirely disenfranchised from the market. Competition ensures the integrity of money production, with minters, money storage facilities, and banks that deceive their customers being pushed out of business by bankruptcy and bank runs. Therefore, while decentralized money production may have problems in individual cases, it does not suffer overall from fraud. As long as consumers have choices, money production is protected from total malfeasance. However, the situation changes when one entity monopolizes the market, exploiting its position by forcing all market participants to endure their transgressions. As the desire to expand wealth without limits appears to be the ultimate goal, competition for financial supremacy has existed since the beginning of human civilization.

Let us acknowledge that states and their monopoly on money production exist in our world, despite the fact that we will later question their purpose and challenge their existence. A government has two primary sources of revenue that it can use to sustain itself. Firstly, it can tax its citizens, but this is a double-edged sword that must be used judiciously. As the government is given legitimacy by its citizens, it must be careful not to antagonize them. Therefore, governments prefer a more discreet method of financing, namely inflation or counterfeiting. When the government creates new money, it profits because not all prices in the economy immediately adjust to the new money supply. Consequently, states have a strong interest in monopolizing the money production market to become the sole beneficiaries of the proceeds from inflation.

However, how can a government monopolize the money market? As they are endorsed by the public, governments can not secretly infringe upon their citizens, similar to how money warehouse operators evolved into bankers. Instead, they need to persuade their constituents through effective propaganda that they hold the authority to engage in widespread theft, and anyone who challenges this is hostile toward the government and unfaithful to their nation. The primary strategy of the government is to outcompete the coinage market through legislation, which is then enforced by the public executive branch. The state essentially gives itself exclusive privileges, which in turn designate it as the only entity authorized to produce money and dictate what money truly is. This set of rights also guarantees that forgery is a crime when committed by others, but not when the state itself engages in counterfeiting. Utilizing these laws, the government can fuel its propaganda campaign and convince the public that it is within its rights as a hegemon to take from them. Thus, by eliminating choices for its citizens, the state lays the groundwork for institutionalized exploitation of its position.

So, what do these individual laws accomplish in promoting inflation? Let's examine how someone might establish a complex inflation machine to generate profit on a large scale at the expense of society.

**Law I - Only the state can counterfeit:** First, let's examine the law that allows only the state to create counterfeit money without consequences. For instance, if a gold coin claims to hold one ounce of gold but contains only half as much gold or none at all, it is still considered worth one ounce of gold by the government. However, this law only applies to government-produced money. If any other party were to create money privately and use it in the economy, they would face severe punishment. While this law may appear unfair, it does potentially offer a significant convenience benefit for all market participants. As every coin with the same imprint is theoretically valued equally, whether debased or not, people supposedly no longer need to confirm its contents and authenticity. However, this is not even true in a closed economy. The market isn't easily deceived, and just because a law states all coins are equal, debased or not, doesn't make them so. As mentioned earlier, in a natural economy, various types of money emerge (such as gold for large transactions, silver for medium-sized ones, and copper for daily life), and people treat them accordingly. Thus, less debased coins are valued higher, and it's probable that they would be removed from circulation as people use them for savings, wealth protection, or sale in foreign markets if possible. Therefore, the right to counterfeit alone doesn't enable inflationary efforts.

**Law II - Only the state can create money:** Second, let's explore the law that allows only the state to create money, thereby eliminating competition. In a hypothetical scenario where a government bans gold as a form of money and decrees that copper coins are the official currency, this would likely impact the demand for these metals in the economy. However, the government can only dictate what is officially considered money; it cannot prevent market participants from evaluating that money based on its intrinsic value. If citizens notice coin debasement or realize that certificates aren't backed by sufficient commodity value, they may reject the government-issued money or redeem it for the underlying commodity. This means that a monopoly on money production alone doesn't necessarily lead to continuous revenue from inflation. While a government can potentially gain some short-term benefits from such a monopoly, it may not be sustainable in the long run.

**Law III - The state forces its subjects to accept its coin:** This brings us to the final option of turning any monetary asset into legal tender as a last resort for the state to enable inflationary theft. Legal tender laws nullify private contracts and require market participants to accept payment in any currency labeled as legal tender. If a loan is issued in gold units and the debtor agrees to repay the lender in gold ounces upon the due date, but silver becomes legal tender in the meantime, the creditor must also accept silver as debt repayment. Naturally, no conflict arises because gold will establish a natural exchange rate for silver in the market. Yet, if the ruling party sets a fixed exchange rate for silver and gold below the natural rate, the debtor can take advantage of the creditor and repay less value than initially agreed upon. Suppose the market rate for one ounce of gold is 20 ounces of silver, but the government sets the exchange rate at 15 ounces instead of 20. In this case, the creditor must accept a smaller payment to settle the loan, as gold is undervalued compared to silver. Accordingly, gold will leave circulation because each gold coin spent represents an undervalued asset. Instead, it will be sold in foreign markets to obtain the complete natural value of 20 ounces of silver. As a result, the silver supply inflates beyond the natural amount demanded, and the gold supply quickly vanishes. The temporary reduction in the overall money supply causes a sharp drop in the price level and harms businesses, as debtors won't be able to pay their debts with lower cash flows. Thus, the local economy suffers from a wave of bankruptcies. During the readjustment process, the government can profit by selling gold at higher rates abroad and paying off its debts at lower costs. As a result, the ability to declare any asset as legal tender enables the government to expand its inflationary measures.

In conclusion, the exclusive authority to define money and to lawfully create counterfeit currency does not enable the government to secure a steady income through inflation because citizens might still assess the value of commodity money and refuse it if necessary. It is only when the government implements legal tender regulations, compelling its constituents to accept devalued money as payment, that it can transform inflation into a source of revenue.

In the end, the government's sinister plan may not appear impressive due to its simplicity rather than complexity. However, maybe that is what makes it so brilliant? By creating laws that protect themselves from any weaknesses in their monopolistic tactics and exerting these laws through violence, society gradually forgets how these regulations were initially validated and begins to accept them as they are. As a result, our currency is now referred to as fiat money, symbolizing money by government decree. While the government's tactic of hiding in plain sight might be malicious, it is undeniably astute. At the very least, nobody can claim they were uninformed!

Nonetheless, while tricking the public might be beneficial, if it leads to a significantly weakened economy and a reduced possibility for prosperity through commerce, the long-term credibility of the state is at risk since it relies on its citizens' goodwill. Therefore, declaring an inferior monetary commodity as legal tender not only results in economic hardship but also carries additional drawbacks, as it poses an economic danger to business people. Merchants and traders tend to stay away from countries where the government is known to devalue the local currency, as there is always a chance of receiving lesser value for their goods than expected in the market. Moreover, governments prone to devaluation have a more challenging time securing more credit and ultimately have to acknowledge that taxes will be paid with the devalued currency. As a result, governments are encouraged to secretly devalue their commodity money.

# Fractional Reserve Banking to Cloak Theft

If governments struggle with inflation that is evident to those affected, why not make it more difficult for the public to understand the situation? One approach is for the government to collect all commodity money by force and then introduce fractional monetary certificates that are not backed by the full value of the commodity. With no way to see the number of certificates in circulation, the government could increase the supply as it wishes, as long as it maintains its ability to exchange certificates for commodity money. This approach requires a fractional reserve banking system to support the plan of hiding the inflationary process in plain sight. But why would the public accept these certificates in the first place? Let's find out.

As previously mentioned, when an inferior or devalued currency is made legal tender, the economy undergoes deflation because the inaccurately valued coins are removed from circulation, leading to a monetary gap. Subsequently, prices must fall such that the entire economy can be measured in the remaining money supply. At this point, governments can step in and fill the gap with fractional paper money certificates supported by the legal tender currency. This idea will be readily accepted by the public, allowing prices to gradually climb again as the money supply expands and economic discomfort diminishes. It's crucial to acknowledge that the government doesn't have to fear the complete redemption of all certificates at once, as long as it exhibits restraint in debasement. Therefore, individual requests for precious metal redemptions can be met. The government's only responsibility is to ensure that the average citizen believes everything is under control, meaning not everybody wants to exchange their paper money certificates for tangible commodities all at once. Ultimately, by eliminating the public's ability to directly observe the amount of legal tender currency in circulation, the government gains control over inflation.

To better comprehend this scenario, let's imagine Sieglandia, a country with 1000 kilograms of gold, 500 kilograms of silver, and 1500 kilograms of copper circulating as one-ounce coins. The prices of all goods in Sieglandia are determined by the availability of these coins. Now, the government has made gold coins the only legal currency in Sieglandia and introduces exchange rates for gold that are lower than the natural rate. As a result, all prices in the economy must adjust due to the exit of silver and copper coins from the market, as they become undervalued. With fewer coins available to price all goods, the only solution is to lower the price of individual goods. Reduced prices lead to economic difficulties because of miscalculations. If the government collects all 1000 kilograms of gold coins and issues paper money certificates instead, no one can verify the number of paper claims on gold, allowing the government to print more certificates than it has gold for redemption. This is only possible when the underlying commodity is separated from the money certificate. If gold is exchanged directly, all prices must represent the presence of gold; however, prices do not need to reflect gold if no one can directly observe the amount of available gold. This plan succeeds as long as the public believes there is a sufficient amount of gold for redemption.

Thus, governments can bypass the negative consequences of making commodity-based currency legal tender by implementing a layer of abstraction through money certificates and establishing them as legal tender. In this manner, the money supply doesn't shrink, preventing a deflationary price spiral and ensuring the domestic economy remains stable. International trade can still use commodity money if needed, creditors aren't deceived, allowing the government to continue accruing debt, and future tax revenues aren't reduced.

It becomes clear why the complex partnership between the government and banks has developed into the formidable force it is today. Banking is safeguarded by the government through legal tender laws, and the government acquires an additional source of revenue. From this point on, the objective is to accumulate wealth through inflationary thievery, limited only by the public's faith in certificate redeemability. Although this final hurdle prevents limitless riches, the government and banks have made significant progress and devised a strategy that allows them to expand their illicit operations.

However, the fractional reserve banking system presents its own challenges, which the Machiavellian government has to address. It appears that banks are poorly motivated and receive rewards for taking on greater risks instead of operating a stable business. Since a bank profits from inflation, it is encouraged to issue more credit and decrease its reserves as much as possible. It is crucial to note that even a prudent banker must keep pace with his ambitious counterparts to maintain his market share. Banks understand that they can only fail if all depositors simultaneously want to redeem their money certificates, and they recognize that other banks are also heavily leveraged and lack sufficient reserves to redeem all paper claims. As a result, banks deduce that if a bank run were to happen on one bank, the banking industry likely supports the individual bank and bail it out to avoid a domino effect. If one bank collapses and sets off a series of bankruptcies, the business clients of other banks may also fail as their customers have just gone bankrupt. If these other clients begin redeeming their money certificates due to crisis concerns, the entire system risks collapse.

As a result, every bank strives to assume more risk to increase profits and maintain their position in the market share race, knowing that they will probably be bailed out in the end. This mutual reliance and coordination requirement has led to the cartelization of the banking industry, with a select few players influencing the financial world. For the government, it is logical to act as a kingmaker, as seen in the earlier case of choosing which commodity to use as a monetary asset, and grant one bank the unique privilege of money production, collaborating with this bank to establish its inflation scheme. This gave rise to the idea of a central bank. The money certificates issued by the central bank will outperform all other money certificates from other banks, and the market will consolidate around the central bank. Strangely enough, the monopoly status and legal protection by the government put the central bank at a disadvantage in comparison to other commercial banks, despite being the sole entity allowed to produce money. Why? Because all other banks depend on the cash it produces, it must maintain larger reserves than commercial banks and cannot issue money certificates as liberally.

# Paper Money to the Moon

We have now arrived at a stage where the government has set up a central bank to manage its inflation strategies and eliminated the use of underlying commodities, like precious metals, in daily transactions with paper currency. As a result, governments can systematically and institutionally exploit this to their advantage. The system may falter if too many people try to exchange their certificates for precious metals due to increasing uncertainties, such as war, but this risk can be lessened by suspending payments - meaning, refusing to swap paper money for commodity money. If a commercial fractional reserve bank were to cease payments in a free market, depositors consider the bank insolvent and avoid it in the future. However, what happens when a central bank stops payments? Does it face the same fate? It is clear that governments strive to prevent the repercussions of their currency's collapse at all costs, like being barred from international trade or experiencing a substantial decrease in their ability to accumulate public debt, while still wanting to inflate the money supply. To solve this dilemma, we must ask: How can a government prevent reaching the point where it has to suspend payments in the first place?

One might expect a complicated web of deceit, but the simple answer lies in adding another layer of deception to the monetary pyramid. What if there were no precious metals to be exchanged for the paper money certificates? What if the paper in your hand truly held value? In this situation, the government can "print" money endlessly, without needing to sustain the illusion of redeemability in precious metals, since the production costs of paper money are virtually nonexistent compared to the labor needed for refining precious metals. Usually, under the cover of national emergencies like war efforts, governments can "temporarily" suspend the conversion of commodities to money certificates.

However, as is commonly known, nothing is more enduring than a temporary government measure. It is important to note that the holders of national monetary certificates - that is, the citizens - have no means of avoiding their fate. Their realistic options include either initiating a revolution to overthrow the government, or withdrawing financial support by determining that paper without commodity backing isn't money and consequently using an alternative commodity as a monetary asset. Given that both options take time to execute and the country is typically amidst a crisis, as previously mentioned, citizens are more inclined to simply accept their new reality. The unfortunate reality is that in the short term, it doesn't matter to them whether or not they accept paper bills at face value to keep the party going and avoid further difficulties. As the connection between money certificates and their underlying commodities has already been severed, it is simpler to participate in a collective delusion of attributing value to paper, rather than facing a significant loss in savings or initiating a revolution. Thus, if everyone believes that paper is money, it becomes a socioeconomic phenomenon. As a result, paper money holds value because the state claims it does and society accepts this difficult truth.

Nonetheless, the long-term consequences experienced by citizens are far more serious. The desire to do and consume more than limited resources allow is not only present in individuals, but also evident in the nature of the state. Personally, we access debt to augment our means to achieve desired outcomes. However, our capacity to borrow money depends on the assets we can provide as collateral to secure a loan. This formula does not apply as readily to the state. When money is simply printed on paper, and the government has no reason to fear rebellion when it inflates the money supply because redeemability is irrelevant, then the government has, in a very literal sense, unrestricted authority to finance all its ventures without the approval of its constituents.

These ventures are nevertheless constrained in scope. The government can print money, but this does not magically create weapons and tanks. The economy still possesses the same resources as before. Considering this, if the government were to endlessly increase the money supply, the only result is a rise in prices. If prices increase too quickly, it can lead to hyperinflation - that is, if money loses its purchasing power daily, or even hourly. Imagine a scenario where a loaf of bread costs $5 in the morning and $20 in the evening at the same store. In such cases, economic reasoning is no longer applicable, and society is likely to cease utilizing the monetary asset until stability is restored.

As a result, although governments can use inflation to fund some of their needs, they cannot be overly aggressive in pursuing this approach if they want to maintain their dominant status. For this reason, they must also employ debt as a means to finance their expenditures. Thus, another constraint emerges in the form of competition among nations, which hampers the sinister plot of granting unlimited monetary authority to any single state. If there were only one country in existence, all market players would have no choice but to accept its monetary manipulation. However, even in our hypothetical scenario, other countries must be acknowledged, and as a result, investors have the choice to invest their money in the public debt of different nations. If a government is notorious for aggressively inflating or for having currency that is only as valuable as the paper it's printed on, then it struggles to raise capital. This implies that national governments must operate their inflationary strategies within certain acceptable limits in order to attract investments. The observant reader might question why anyone lends money to a government known for perpetrating such theft. The apparent answer is accurate in this instance: because the investor stands to benefit from it as well. As discussed earlier, if a government increases the money supply, prices within the economy will rise, causing assets such as real estate and company stocks to also appreciate in value. Who owns the majority of these assets? Primarily investors, rather than the average citizen. Consequently, society must contend with rising living costs, but usually, their wages do not increase as rapidly as asset price inflation. So, even though investors are aware that governments inflate the money supply and profit from it, they also stand to gain as they become relatively wealthier compared to the rest of society, ultimately improving their overall situation.

In conclusion, we have discovered that governments have an insatiable desire for revenue, which can be fulfilled either by imposing higher taxes on citizens or through inflation. Increasing taxes is unfavorable and undermines the state's legitimacy; therefore, the hidden force of inflation has always been the favored method of theft. Natural money sets a boundary on rampant inflation, as the money certificate is intrinsically linked to the underlying commodity. However, once the certificate is separated from its represented value, the door is opened for fractional reserve banking to further escalate the inflationary scheme. Governments and banks can use inflation as a limitless source of revenue only after the implementation of legal tender laws. These laws provide the authority to create money and control its supply, allowing them to generate profits without boundaries. The adoption of paper currency, which possesses no intrinsic value, allows the government to assert its control over money creation and dodge any accountability to its people when making decisions. If you are reading this book and living in a democratic country, have you ever questioned why you cannot vote for the individual who heads the central bank? This person arguably holds the most critical position in any economic system and can instantly eradicate your financial assets. Why, then, is such an influential role not subject to democratic election?

# Statism

If governments and states are such burdens on society, why do we allow them to persist? If you acknowledge that you are being robbed daily, you make every effort to alter this circumstance. Nonetheless, under the guise of patriotism and the continuous effort to stay afloat amid rising inflation, we fail to question the fundamental structure of our society. Instead, we passively accept the existing conditions, much like heroin addicts who prioritize their impulses over logic. Humanity never takes a moment to step back and reflect upon the reality we observe.

It's all too easy to dismiss any opposition to the state because it shapes the world around us and constantly reinforces its necessity through our everyday experiences. If the state is responsible for all infrastructure, streets, laws, police, and various other services, it's difficult to envision a different way of life. However, just because our present world is governed by statism, it doesn't imply that it has to stay that way. Keep in mind, there is a difference between knowledge gained through observation (our current reality) and knowledge obtained through reasoning (possible reality). To dismiss knowledge derived from reason, as our current economic system does, is intellectually dishonest. If all men mistreated women on a regular basis, does that mean that the reality for these women is the only feasible existence, simply because it's confirmed by daily observation? Clearly, the answer is no. Therefore, let us explore the genesis of statism, assess its consequences, and evaluate the path that states embark upon, potentially leading us towards a grim future.

## The Emergence of Nation States

Even in a hypothetical state of nature, where individuals exist without the constraints of law and order, humans are restricted by the limited availability of resources, leading to the necessity of making choices. We cannot perform multiple tasks at once, and two people cannot occupy the exact same space simultaneously. If John consumes the last chocolate piece in the refrigerator, Jane cannot have it as well, despite her desire for it. Consequently, conflicts arise between human beings when our intended actions clash.

One might assume that in such a situation, the law of the jungle prevails, with the physically stronger individual holding a monopoly on violence and, therefore, imposing their will. However, let us debunk this misconception for a moment. What do you think occurs if the stronger person consistently imposes their will on weaker individuals? Others soon learn to avoid that person, resulting in their isolation. While subjugating others is advantageous in the short term, it becomes burdensome if it's required in every interaction. As a result, violence becomes costly for the one who exerts it. Moreover, if the strong individual is ostracized from trade and society, their life will be considerably more challenging than if they lived harmoniously with others. Hence, predatory behavior, manifested in cannibalism, slavery, and crime, may provide short-term benefits but is unsustainable in the long run. Humanity quickly realizes that cooperation is more advantageous than violence.

If not through violence, how should conflicts be resolved? To address this issue, individuals recognize the necessity for an arbitrator: a person or institution that resolves disputes based on universally accepted laws for those seeking to live within that society. Similar to the intrinsic value of natural commodity money, an arbitrator cannot be chosen by force. Society must perceive the arbitrator as deserving of their role through the respect of their peers. This respect may be earned through exceptional skill, wealth, or military accomplishments. The arbitrator must possess a natural authority that the majority of society accepts, enabling them to have the final say in dispute resolution. If the arbitrator were in their position solely by force, they are no different than the initial strongman and are expelled from society. Additionally, abuse of power results in their removal by the public. Though imagining such a society requires a fair amount of faith, consider the dynamics in kindergarten and elementary school. While adults usually established some rules, children naturally developed their social hierarchy and norms without a single child acting as the playground's dictator. Since children's behavior is based more on instinct than elaborate thought, their actions closely resemble a natural societal state without centrally imposed power.

Consequently, the most natural form of human society is an aristocracy, where its leaders are chosen based on merit and validated by public respect.

In this set up, aristocratic nobles act as mediators, and their judgments can be disputed in the courts overseen by other nobles. If they were to err, they must take responsibility for their mistakes, unlike the (democratic) state, whose judgments cannot be contested, even if erroneous. However, disputes must ultimately be resolved, as one can imagine two parties constantly resorting to various noble courts to resolve their conflict until one of them stops and accepts the judgment. Hence, the concept of a king arises, who serves as a noble amongst nobles and the final arbitrator of the law. It is important to note that in this society, the king has no extra privileges compared to others. He must abide by the prevailing universal law like everyone else, cannot establish new laws on a whim, and has no special rights to levy taxes or confiscate land. Every individual is a king on their own property and enjoys equal privileges in society. Kings are not born into their position but become kings through acceptance and can be replaced if required.

So, how can a king accumulate power and turn into a constitutional monarch with the authority to impose taxes and become not just the protector but also the creator of universal law? The answer lies in human nature, which can be driven by baser instincts. In every society, there are inevitably the 'haves' and the 'have-nots' - people who choose the easy way out and those who embrace hardships to attain wealth and power. While a free society allows everyone to attain higher social status through hard work, many find this too uncomfortable and would rather blame wealthy individuals for their misfortunes. Kings exploit the common people's bitterness towards the aristocrats and form alliances with them. By convincing the common people to support the king, he would assure them that he could make their lives easier by seizing lands from the nobles and forgiving their debts owed to the nobles. In return, the people would have to accept the king as their rightful lawgiver and pay taxes to finance the king's efforts against the "evil" aristocracy. To most ordinary individuals, this seems like a good deal, and soon, kings are legitimized not by merit but by laws they created themselves. Consequently, they monopolize the market for lawmaking and arbitration. To consolidate their power, kings appoint former aristocrats, stripped of their assets, as key figures in their court, ensuring their loyalty and preventing revolt. Additionally, kings enlist intellectuals to create an ideology and propaganda machine that portray the pre-kingdom world as chaotic. Thus, the world forgets the original concept of kings being legitimized by merit, and these rulers come to govern their subjects without constraints.

If the call for equality can persuade the masses once, it can do so again. As every individual believes they are deserving of more, it becomes clear how having power concentrated in the hands of one person can lead to the desire for that person's downfall. In this way, the intellectuals, consumed by their own zeal, believe they are the legitimate representatives for the ordinary people, and it is they who should rightfully control the laws and government in the interest of equality. As a result, the rulers become victims of the very jealousy that initially raised them to their positions of power, and the ordinary citizens are embodied by those who can most skillfully allure them with false promises and well-meaning schemes designed to enhance their lives. And so, democracy is born, and for the common people, the trade-off is easy to accept. They reap immediate benefits at the cost of sacrificing a single family – a small price to pay! However, they fail to consider the consequences of having no one accountable for a nation's long-term success. While it may seem that having equal standing before the law and positions without privilege in government are akin to a natural aristocracy, the reality is quite different. Judgments can no longer be challenged in other courts, and the law is no longer universally accepted but rather a product of the government.

In conclusion, states form out of the necessity to settle disputes among human beings. Regrettably, human nature is easily manipulated when emotions take precedence. Collectively, we tend to prioritize short-term gains over long-term benefits. For this reason, people as a group become easy targets for swindlers who make grand promises, only to deliver little of value. As a result, our history is peppered with stories of kings and democratic leaders, but there are far fewer accounts of truly free societies.

# Implications of the Democratic State

From the viewpoint of the prevalent Western democratic ideology, it seems unthinkable that any political structure other than democracy should be considered valid. However, upon closer analysis, it is evident that the shift from aristocracy to monarchy and eventually to democracy leads to numerous negative consequences that did not exist before. In a democratic system, the main issue is that the separation between the rulers and the ruled does not disappear; instead, it becomes even more noticeable. Historically, the monarch held exclusive power in determining who was part of the ruling class and who could take advantage of the public. This group was relatively small, as the monarch aimed to accumulate maximum power. Conversely, democracies attempt to broaden their authority by incorporating public officials who claim to protect the people but ultimately lead to further exploitation through taxation and regulations. Since anyone can theoretically join the ruling class, the public is less opposed to democracy because, in theory, anyone can access public wealth.

Moreover, in a democracy, the redistribution of wealth and income often appears to be an appealing and beneficial practice. However, it inevitably results in reduced motivation to innovate and produce. Monarchs are more inclined to respect and reward achievers, while democracies transfer wealth from the prosperous to the unproductive. This subsequently fosters bad habits and reliance on redistributed income, ultimately leading to an impoverished society with a diminished quality of life. Critics might question what occurs if a debauched individual becomes ruler - someone who enjoys torture, exploitation, and violence? The issue likely works itself out. The royal family has a vested interest in preserving their social position and does not jeopardize their standing for the whim of a deranged ruler. As a result, the reign of a mad ruler is brief, as accidents are ever-present threats.

Additionally, the popularity-based apparatus for ascending to power in democracies tends to favor the unscrupulous over the temperate, promoting the very type of person who exploits their constituents. Consequently, the lowest in character rise to the pinnacle of the social hierarchy, and the instruments of mass exploitation, such as taxation and inflation, fall into the hands of those who have little consideration for the overall wellbeing of their electorate. For example, monarchs usually adopt a more balanced approach to taxation, contemplating the long-term ramifications of such decisions on productivity. This means they act to guarantee that their accrued debt does not grow too quickly, conscious of the implications excessive borrowing may have on future generations. In opposition, democratic representatives often accumulate debt without any assurance of repayment, as they are not personally accountable for it. Generally, monarchs prioritize capital conservation, while democracies emphasize immediate consumption.

Hence, the evolution of the predominant political framework from a natural aristocracy, through monarchy, and finally to democracy can be characterized as a progressive increase in the time preference of those who govern - in other words, the prioritization of immediate satisfaction over long-term rewards. As a consequence, the quality of the decisions made by the ruling class has progressively worsened over time, as their decision-making increasingly centers on the present at the expense of the future.

What occurs when the present continually takes precedence over the future? Unfavorable outcomes are bound to happen. If we constantly opt for consuming chips now rather than exercising later, we put on weight. If we choose immediate sexual gratification instead of waiting for a few dates, we can become perpetrators. If we select working and earning money now rather than obtaining a university degree, we may be excluded from highly-paid job opportunities. If we persistently give in to the temptation of consuming alcohol or taking drugs, we never achieve a sober lifestyle. And most importantly, if we never start saving money and accumulating capital, we'll be forced to take on growing amounts of debt to satisfy our wants.

An aristocrat, serving as a dispute resolver, lacks motivation for self-serving interests. Recognizing that the public has access to multiple judicial systems in an aristocratic society, the mediator is aware that their clients always possess alternative choices. As a result, leaning towards short-sighted decisions is not advantageous, and they must ensure clients feel their rights are respected. Additionally, they acknowledge that they too might need to rely on a legal system in the future. For this reason, they endeavor to maintain the highest standards of justice and prevent any form of misconduct. Thus, natural leaders and aristocrats display a low time preference, with their actions reflecting their consideration for the future and restraint in pursuing present desires.

Being a king is a different matter. If a king encounters legal difficulties, he is likely to face defeat since the court is under another ruler's jurisdiction who may aim to annex the territory. Therefore, a king does not have to comply with the rule of law in his court, as he embodies the law. With this in mind, a king's incentives shift from focusing on societal well-being to centering on the welfare of his monarchy and royal lineage. Kings endeavor to retain their power and secure the long-term prosperity of their heirs. Although kings may make choices motivated by self-interest, they at least take their family's well-being into account. As such, they preserve a certain level of law enforcement and steer clear of accumulating debt without suitable supervision. In terms of time preference, we can assert that kings demonstrate a moderate level of time preference; they act in the present while bearing the future in mind.

Delving deeper in analyzing the contemporary political incentive structure, it becomes apparent that we have made a mistake if we consider elected democratic leaders to be superior to aristocrats or monarchs in terms of long-term decision-making, adhering to high judicial standards, or demonstrating fiscal responsibility. Since politicians have limited terms, they need to showcase their accomplishments in order to secure re-election. As a result, there is a higher probability of making choices based on popularity rather than selecting the appropriate ones. In order to fund their desired projects, democratic politicians must save money like any other economic participant. However, most politicians seem to find reasons why the present situation is unfavorable for saving, leading to a continual growth of debt. The same applies to the legal system. Governments preserve current legislation and enact new ones supporting their objectives, progressively providing them with increased authority. As a result, democrats display a high time preference, implementing decisions presently without pondering the eventual repercussions. They prioritize the present rather than the future, due to the fact that their term of office is finite, and unlike monarchs, their children will not immediately assume their positions.

In terms of time preference, we can liken aristocracy, monarchy, and democracy to a rational adult, an emotional adolescent, and an infant who solely relies on instincts and immediate gratification, respectively. The lingering question is whether we genuinely wish to be governed by infantile instincts?

## The State's Natural Path to War

The central issue that every advocate of nations and democracy must address is the ultimate outcome of statism. What is the reason for having multiple states and countries instead of just one? States are in competition with one another, and to ensure their survival, they must expand at the expense of other states or be consumed by a larger one. As a result, statism is inherently prone to expansion and must attempt to grow its revenue base either through inflation or taxes to fund its attacks on other states. It's important to note that this process is not voluntary, and even if a specific state has no desire to annex other states, other states will be motivated to take over the state in question. Consequently, the peaceful state must also increase its revenue base to protect itself. No state is immune from the battle for survival. Thus, the rise of statism sets us on a path of total warfare until only one state remains.

Our Western democratic ideology teaches us that democracy is humanity's ultimate peace-bringer while depicting previous eras as brutal periods of constant human conflict. However, the reality is that only since the advent of democracy and the centralization of monetary production under the state's control have wars become more significant in terms of victims and human suffering. The formula yielding this outcome is quite straightforward: unlimited resources obtained through inflationary theft and ideologically driven conflicts rather than quarrels based on specific disputes. Though it may appear somewhat extreme to label democracy as a war instigator instead of a peacemaker, it is undeniably accurate.

Before nation-states came into existence, wars were fought between realms due to disagreements and conflicts over territory, politics, and resources. The crucial distinction is that these wars were waged between rulers, not ordinary people. Rulers regarded their citizens as possessions, and warring with their citizens resulted in destroying their own property. Thus, rulers primarily employed mercenary armies that faced each other on the battleground and resolved the dispute. As soon as one side recognized they lost the battle, they immediately ceased fighting. No one could afford to shed too much blood, and the defeated ruler had to accept their fate. Furthermore, the capacity to wage war was constrained by the need for rulers to collect taxes to fund their military campaigns. It was easier to collect taxes for defensive purposes when another ruler attempted to invade their territory. The ruler's subjects understood that their ruler sought to safeguard their land, so he could persuade the public to finance his aims. Conversely, collecting taxes for offensive military campaigns proved much more difficult. The local population had nothing to gain from the realm's expansion, as paying war taxes meant supporting the ruler's efforts to amass property. Rulers could not excessively raise taxes; otherwise, they risked being overthrown by the public or assassinated by their family for fear of revolt against their rule. While they could debase the currency supply and fund wars through inflation, as we have seen earlier, commodity money cannot be debased quickly, limiting this option. Thus, leaders were directly responsible for their choices concerning warfare, and they viewed themselves as the kingdom's owners who depended on the backing of the populace to accomplish their goals. These elements kept wars from spiraling out of control or turning into endless pursuits. Every conflict had a well-defined goal from the beginning and ended in either triumph or loss. Warfare was only entered into when strictly essential and used the minimum resources required, as rulers were not inclined to destroy their source of revenue or possessions. As a result, wars were measured undertakings rather than self-sustaining ventures.

Conversely, the constraints that once limited kings vanished with the rise of statism. Nowadays, national leaders serve as temporary representatives rather than nation owners. Therefore, presidents and chancellors regard their countries not as property, but as vehicles for personal glory and wealth, since they are not immediately accountable for their actions' repercussions. Moreover, the capacity to print and inflate money significantly fuels the fact that democracies can maintain wars longer than monarchies. War expenditures are not transparent through taxes; instead, they are transferred as hidden fees via inflation. As a result, the government does not have to worry about insurrection since most citizens remain indifferent to war, provided it stays far from home. With this distinct motivation structure and broadened war financing methods, the nature of warfare has drastically shifted. Wars are now fueled by ideological motives rather than just resolving conflicts. The US openly strives to spread democracy worldwide and intervenes in numerous global military matters. By vilifying nations that reject their principles, the US purchases domestic support for war with propaganda, as the vast majority remain unaware that their government uses inflation to impoverish them. War has evolved into a comprehensive means to enrich the political elite via inflation, rather than a simple dispute resolution mechanism.

It becomes apparent that statism paves the way for all-out war as resources dwindle and Western and Eastern ideologies collide. To celebrate statism and democracy as harbingers of peace is utterly superficial, considering the reality is quite the opposite. The advent of nuclear power and atomic weapons has led the world to a deadlock, offering no release without considerable human anguish. The influence of atomic bombs on today's boundaries remains contested. These weapons enable smaller nations to protect themselves against more powerful ones; in their absence, larger countries would have gradually assimilated smaller ones resulting in the survival of just one single state.

Consequently, the US has transitioned from physical imperialism to financial imperialism. They have acknowledged that exporting the dollar and promoting their democratic ideals allows for empire expansion without resorting to military action. However, war is still war, regardless of whether it involves physical or digital weaponry and the previous century has witnessed no other nation as merciless and triumphant in its growth as the US.

# Anarchy

Is it possible to halt the natural progression of war driven by the insatiable thirst for power of nation-states? Indeed, it is. However, to address this matter, we must first explore what the alternative would involve. A logical starting point to tackle this issue is to consider the potential outcome if humanity had not given in to the aspirations and false promises of manipulative individuals who declared themselves kings, whose eventual downfall facilitated the rise of nation-states. In essence, what would a world without states look like? If we can successfully create a stateless society, we can avoid the horrors associated with statism. We can approach the issue from two distinct viewpoints: either by envisioning an alternate world based on a moral framework of reason and justice, or by examining the influence of market forces.

## Anarchy Based on Morals

Reconstructing a society without central authority from an ethical standpoint emphasizes that the primary objective is achieving justice, not economic gain. In order to peacefully coexist, everyone needs to adhere to the same laws. This means that rationality must prevail over emotions. Consequently, the initial question of how we interact with each other evolves into, "What is equitable and just for everyone?" A just system is the only one universally accepted within a society. The question of whether this system yields the greatest economic output is secondary to the primary concern of fairness.

Earlier we established that the ideal starting point is an axiom - a self-evident truth that forms a solid basis for reasoning. From there, we build our arguments to shape the society we want, whether it be anarchy, capitalism, socialism, or even communism. Despite the objections of socialist-leaning free spirits and harmony advocates, the only viable method for creating a morally sound society from its original state of nature involves embracing libertarian principles of private property.

To grasp this concept, it's crucial to realize that we must engage in meaningful conversations with one another to reach an agreement about our future society. Achieving consensus requires dialogue, which in turn depends on the use of limited resources and the recognition of an individual's exclusive control over their body. Otherwise, everyone could switch bodies and speak for others. Furthermore, the notion of scarcity must be considered. Since we cannot simultaneously engage in various activities like having sex, playing tennis, drinking vermouth, racing cars, and reading on the beach, we also cannot advocate for anarchy, democracy, monarchy, aristocracy, communism, and fascism all at once. Thus, it becomes clear that each person's arguments are their personal property, and they must choose which ones to present.

Rejecting the concept of private property is untenable, as doing so would only validate its existence. Following this line of reasoning, we must accept and respect the principle of private property as the underpinning for any argument or idea to be valid. Just as it is impossible to win a game of chess without adhering to its rules, no ethical claim can be substantiated without recognizing the ethics of private property. As a result, accepting the ethics of private property will guide us toward a world where humans coexist harmoniously, unencumbered by the weight of state control, because it is the only ethic whose inherent laws can be morally justified. But how can we be sure of this?

By recognizing the concept of property, we quickly understand that we cannot truly possess an object but only have the ownership rights to that object. When we transfer these rights to another person, the ownership status shifts. Therefore, one can only acquire property through production, which involves blending one's labor with raw materials, or through exchanging produced goods (gifts are also included in this category). If I neither create something nor exchange something I produced for another item and instead steal it, my actions are immoral, as I have taken away another person's labor. Likewise, I can voluntarily sell my labor capabilities for money or goods. No one can force me to sell my labor, and I cannot force someone to accept my labor in exchange for their goods. Thus, a free society is based on the voluntary exchange of goods and services produced by combining labor with resources among its members. In such a society, any act of aggression - for example, imposing one's will on another person through violence - is considered an intrusion of private property. As a result, the natural law of liberty is the only valid ethic for humanity, as it applies universally and supports self-ownership for all individuals.

It is crucial to recognize that the moral perspective on private property laws, involving the fundamental right to self-ownership and autonomy, may result in controversial consequences based on the prevailing ethical theory in Western society. This theory adheres to the utilitarian principle, which contends that actions should aim to benefit the majority of individuals, even at the cost of disregarding individual property rights. For example, the majority of people consider bribery as unethical. Nevertheless, from a moral standpoint, there is nothing intrinsically wrong if neither participant in the bribe was forced into it, rendering it a market transaction like any other.

A more dramatic example involves a misdirected train that would kill five people if it continues on its current track but only kill one person if rerouted to another track. Utilitarianism supports violating the property rights of the one person to save the five potential survivors. In contrast, liberal ethics regard the non-aggression principle as the highest good for society. From this perspective, it is morally unjustifiable to infringe property rights under any circumstance, even due to another person's misfortune. As per this view, the train should not change direction, thus resulting in the death of the five people instead of the one person.

If violence is strictly prohibited in our free society, how should we defend ourselves against those who refuse to adhere to the non-aggression principle? It must be clarified that violence is only forbidden when used offensively, not defensively. Every free individual has the right to protect their property by any means necessary, including weapons and firearms. Consequently, prohibiting guns through legislation is a severe violation of private property, as it takes away the ability to defend oneself. Additionally, it is morally justifiable to reclaim property from a thief who has taken it beforehand. However, this is only ethical if I were the original owner. If I steal something from a thief that I did not own before, I also become a thief, thereby violating the non-aggression principle. In the former case, I am defending myself; in the latter, I am aggressing. Due to this rationale, the deeds of Robin Hood (taking from the wealthy and providing for the underprivileged) may be defensible from an equalitarian standpoint, but they contradict the principles of justice. In fact, Robin Hood is a debased individual with a disregard for personal possession. The act of vigilantism in chasing equality cannot be considered just, but rather egocentric and unlawful.

Although self-defense is not a violent act, it must be executed cautiously and only as a response to an aggressive assault. It is not acceptable, for example, to hit someone who has given you a menacing stare that offended you. Similarly, it is inappropriate to use excessive or disproportional force for defense; for instance, a homeowner cannot kill a burglar for stealing a laptop from their home. These reactions would infringe on the aggressor's rights, as they go beyond what is necessary to shield oneself from an attack. What should be considered justice, and what is the appropriate amount of restitution for the victim then? Today, conventional wisdom perceives the "eye for an eye, tooth for a tooth" principle as barbaric nonsense. However, when considering proportionality in criminal justice without an arbitrary authority dictating and enforcing laws through violence, it makes perfect sense. Why should a criminal be punished more than the severity of their crime? Modern Western justice holds a contrasting view. The foundation of our penal system is built on the belief that the goal is not to punish individuals, but to employ punishment as a means to reform wrongdoers ("rehabilitation"). As a result, states and governments create legal frameworks that view people as "ill" and in need of "therapy" instead of punitive measures. In such a system, a person charged with a minor drug offense may find themselves imprisoned for years, never getting the opportunity to taste freedom once more. What sort of justice can truly be found in such a system?

A more suitable approach is to impose penalties that correspond to the offense ("proportional punishment"). In this way, the victim can obtain the justice they are entitled to, while the punishment remains just for the perpetrator. For example, if John pilfers 1000 USD from Jane, he should return the 1000 USD to her. Additionally, John needs to experience the same anguish as Jane, and therefore must give her an extra 1000 USD as retribution for his transgression. To compensate for the uncertainty Jane encountered throughout the ordeal, a minor additional fee should also be paid by John to mitigate her distress. Consequently, to adequately compensate Jane for the theft of 1000 USD, John has to reimburse her 2200 USD, which may be regarded as justice. However, what is undoubtedly not just is the distortion of rehabilitation as punishment. In this scenario, Jane must pay taxes to the state, which subsequently places John in a facility that rehabilitates him for his misdeed, costing even more in taxes. As a result, Jane pays triple: she does not recoup the stolen money, she bankrolls John's rehabilitation, and she subsidizes the state to maintain the pretense. How can we locate any sense of justice in this procedure? The answer is, we cannot.

The idea of private property and the non-aggression principle quickly reveal states and governments as unlawful violators. Governments forcibly collect taxes without explicit consent. No individual has agreed to a social contract that involves paying taxes in exchange for the services provided by the state. Additionally, there is no option to opt-out. And we have not even discussed the concealed tax of inflation, which violates citizens' property rights every time the government expands the money supply. In conclusion, to rebuild society from its foundations as a free community, adherence to the non-aggression principle and acknowledgment of private property by all individuals is necessary. In a society based on voluntary exchange, no moral principles are undermined, allowing us to coexist justly, implementing the law of proportional retribution to those who violate these principles.

Nonetheless, who is responsible for enforcing the laws? In a stateless society, there wouldn't be a public police force, correct? Although the concepts of private property and non-aggression might be persuasive in theory, is it truly possible for them to work effectively in practice? Or is there a possibility that an individual or organization could monopolize violence, ultimately leading to history repeating itself?

## Anarchy Based on Markets

It is true that a world where logic triumphs over human emotions and everyone adheres to reason seems improbable. However, we don't necessarily need to rely on reason to shape such a world; instead, we can simply embrace individualism and allow market forces to work their magic. So, what would a society look like if it were entirely driven by the resource allocation mechanisms of the market, free from government interference?

What if every person acted solely in their own self-interest? Arguably, playing devil's advocate, one might say that the world would be exactly as it is today, since throughout history, people have always prioritized their own needs over those of others or the broader society. Individuals who support the rise of a king do so out of a desire to alleviate their own debts. The issue here is that they are prioritizing short-term benefits over long-term ones. As such, emotions and irrationality can lead humans to the same position we currently find ourselves in. Nevertheless, history could have taken an alternative path, leading us toward a truly free society. Let's explore what that world might look like and how the market could generate security, law, and order in a stateless society.

We already know that in a world without states, people wouldn't constantly be at each other's throats. Instead, based on the theory of the division of labor, humans would cooperate and offer various benefits to one another within the market. Furthermore, we recognize that there may always be those who believe they are above societal norms and choose to use violence to achieve their goals. Such criminals would be vastly outnumbered by rational individuals who understand that a life of constant conflict is undesirable. Consequently, a demand for protection services against these criminals would emerge within the free market. Like any other commodity, protection could be provided by companies that cater to their clients' needs. This would result in the creation of protection agencies offering a range of security services. These agencies would likely provide differing levels of protection and coverage, allowing them to stand out from their competitors. Customers would then subscribe to a particular service and pay a monthly fee for protection against crime.

The story could end here, but what if both the victim and the perpetrator employ protection agencies to ensure their safety? Suppose person A accuses person B of theft, but person B denies the allegation. Both individuals then seek the assistance of their respective protection agencies, potentially leading to conflict between the two groups. Is violence the only resolution? The answer is no, as economics tells us that violence is costly and ultimately an inefficient solution. Instead, both agencies would opt for a peaceful way to resolve their dispute. This is where private arbitrators become relevant. Just as there is a demand for security services, the market also requires arbitration services to settle such conflicts. These arbitrator companies would provide varying types of laws, designed to cater to different preferences. For example, one might endorse the death penalty for particularly heinous crimes, while another might take a more compassionate approach. Protection agencies would then establish contracts with these arbitrators, agreeing on which laws they will adhere to in resolving disputes. They would market these contracts to their clients, who would choose an agency that aligns with their preferences. Since the consumers pay the protection agencies and the protection agencies pay the arbitrators, the law will exist based on what the consumers have agreed to. Protection agencies and consumers may find it more cost-effective to work within a limited set of laws, leading to a gradual convergence of the lawmaking process in the open market and the emergence of a legal system. Similar to how no two private health insurance policies are identical, the eventual products offered to the market will be comparable enough to be considered as the same offering. Though no arbiter will provide the exact same law, the differences will be subtle enough that consumers will not be confused. A single legal system is unlikely to emerge, as this would make it vulnerable to competition from alternative systems.

Even though this concept may seem absurd and unfair, it aligns more closely with reality than one might think. Different countries have different laws, such as the legality of cannabis in the Netherlands versus that in Saudi Arabia. Even within a single country like the United States, there are varying state laws. Therefore, this proposal is not entirely unprecedented, as we are already familiar with such variations on a larger scale. The key innovation lies in applying the same principle on a smaller scale.

Some perceptive readers might interject, arguing that in such a system, either a rogue group might take over territories (akin to the mafia), or protection agencies might find crime and theft to be more lucrative than providing protection services. If these thoughts were taken to their logical conclusion, larger protection agencies would ultimately consume smaller ones, resulting in a government-like protection agency at the forefront. We can counter both concerns with the same argument: Agencies that resolve conflicts through violence are already at a disadvantage. The economics of brutality are simply too poor. Agencies that use force incur much greater costs than those that settle disputes peacefully with the assistance of arbitrators. Higher costs either result in reduced profitability, which leads to a decline in service quality for clients over time, or increased costs for clients as the agency attempts to recoup its greater expenses. In either case, if clients can obtain the same service elsewhere at a lower cost, they will not tolerate poorer quality or higher fees and will switch agencies. Rogue agencies are defunded more rapidly than they can steal and go bankrupt. Moreover, it will always be more valuable for a victim of aggression to be protected from crime than for a criminal to engage in wrongdoing. As a result, the willingness to pay for protection is higher than the willingness to pay for committing a crime, making it impossible for a single agency to grow and expand through violence. Also, consider that it is highly improbable that all protection agencies would unite and peacefully determine that they now represent the government and control the country, similar to a military coup. Why then do the military and police not wield power in every nation? Briefly stated, people generally act according to what they consider fair and just and recognize when they are doing something wrong. Consequently, accepted social norms prevent them from doing so. Furthermore, in a free society, it is likely that gun ownership is widespread and the vast majority of society is armed. When it comes down to it, people can defend themselves and outnumber any conspiracy's participants. Blood may be spilled, but ultimately, freedom will triumph over rogue actors.

It may take some time to accept the notion that law and order can be market commodities rather than political goods, but it is crucial to contemplate this idea. Why should law be something forced top-down onto society rather than emerging from a bottom-up process? In a free-market society, everyone can use their economic power to vote to achieve a specific goal. Put plainly: one dollar, one vote. Indeed, it is accurate to say that, in theory, the affluent possess an advantage over the impoverished; however, this does not necessarily apply in practical terms. For example, if poor people enjoy using crystal meth but wealthy people do not, the poor value its consumption more than the rich value its prohibition. Therefore, it would cost the affluent substantial economic power to criminalize crystal meth (recall that this would require subscribing to protection services, which would then settle disputes before arbitrators who would declare crystal meth illicit). The rich accumulate wealth not by frivolous spending, but by focusing their resources on what matters to them. As a result, it is more probable that crystal meth would be banned in some areas but allowed in others. If particularly avid crystal meth users were present, they would congregate in one location and legalize the drug (with no disrespect intended towards the poor, as the argument could also be made in reverse with cocaine as the substance of choice), and the wealthy would accept this arrangement as they would not want to reside in such an area anyway. Thus, any grotesque practice would have a place in the world as long as enough people support it. As criminals require punishment rather than rehabilitation, free individuals can decide what they wish to do with their own bodies. They do not need saving if they do not seek salvation. Law and order should concentrate on safeguarding private property and maintaining an orderly market process rather than acting as caretakers and shielding people from themselves. If you truly believe in democracy, you would not agree with the assertion that the law is beyond the decision-making authority of the general public and should be created in secrecy.

## The Tragedy of the Commons is not so Tragic

We have seen that the market, just like with other goods, has the potential to provide law and security. I could now spend countless pages analyzing every possible product and service to determine whether the free market can provide a particular good. However, let us focus on other products we consider to be "public" goods, just like law and safety.

According to contemporary economic theory, public goods are those that the government must provide because market mechanisms fail to deliver them, despite benefiting everyone. The argument then extends to claim that this market failure justifies the existence of governments. But is this actually the case? Is it truly impossible for the market to provide public goods in a broader sense, and if so, does that necessarily require the existence of governments?

Public goods, often referred to as the tragedy of the commons, encompass those goods that benefit everyone and from which nobody can be excluded. Here, the tragedy stems from personal incentives stopping the market from generating these goods. Take a firefighting service, for example. A business owner cannot offer firefighting services solely to customers who pay for it, as fires spread and impact everyone. Consequently, the service must be available to everyone, whether or not they have paid for it. This results in people making the economically rational decision not to pay for the service, as their payment will not make a difference. Ultimately, the market fails to supply the service, even though the value of having a firefighting service for all exceeds the costs of provisioning it. In other words, market failure occurs when individual rationality doesn't lead to collective rationality - when individuals act in their self-interest but don't benefit the group.

The problem worsens when more people reap the benefits of the public good. If everyone benefits, each individual only has a minute contribution to make for the public good to materialize. Hence, no one will donate anything because they assume others will contribute. However, if a small group of people must collaborate, the situation differs. For example, ten people find a way to fund a Wi-Fi tower or find an alternative solution if they genuinely wanted internet access in a remote area. But how can 400 million people living without political governance determine a method for provisioning a national defense service? Since we live without a government and military, it doesn't mean other nations do the same. Therefore, we must protect ourselves not only from internal criminals but also from external threats. National defense may be the most extreme instance of a public good. If it's theoretically possible to supply defense services, then any public good can be provided in a society without a government.

The solution might astonish or even frustrate you, as many intellectuals might not see it as an answer. To address the tragedy of the commons, consider the concept of charity, specifically in the form of tips and donations. We usually tip at restaurants even if they are far from where we live, desiring good service at all locations rather than just a few. The same reasoning applies to national defense. We want our territory to be well-guarded against invaders; therefore, in a stateless society, a mechanism would emerge for us to tip national defense organizations that protect our domain. If this solution appears far-fetched, think about corporate pledges and sponsorships. National defense agencies could secure corporate sponsors, similar to sports clubs, to finance their defense campaigns, consequently enhancing brand visibility and favorable consumer perception. Furthermore, companies could pledge a specific percentage of their profits to national defense, comparable to environmental commitments, and subsequently promote themselves positively. Whilst financing a defense effort through charity might sound contradictory and unfeasible, it might just be the most straightforward solution to the issue.

Therefore, the market is fully capable of providing all the goods society needs without the state as a mediator. Whether you favor a society grounded in private property rights or one based on the existence of markets stemming from the innate need for human cooperation, the essential point is the same. Both perspectives arrive at the conclusion that states are not required to create a framework for harmonious coexistence. People are fully capable of self-organizing through market mechanisms without relying on an entity that exploits its members through the use of force. Anarchy is not synonymous with chaos; rather, it signifies societal order established through market forces.

If you vehemently oppose the concept of charity and tipping as a means to supply national defense services and other public goods that require collaboration among large groups of individuals, I can empathize. However, the necessity of these goods does not establish the legitimacy of the state's existence. By condoning the state, we implicitly support its expansion. Instead, we should identify the state for what it is: a group of thieves and extortionists who terrorize their subjects. Regrettably, if this particular criminal organization shields us from an even more vicious and cruel group seizing control, we have to accept its existence.

It is unfortunate that there has not been an approach to restrict the government's provision of goods solely to those that the market is unable to produce efficiently. As a result, dealing with the expansion of the government has been inevitable since the concept of a restrained government was never a feasible alternative.

This reality will evolve. Let's explore how we can disassociate the production of money from the state to curb its desire for expansion, and subsequently compel it to offer only the most essential goods in terms of property rights protection and arbitration services, thereby validating its existence.

# Bitcoin

Thus far, we have explored the necessity for a medium of exchange in a barter-based society, the corruption of money through numerous layers of deceit as it evolved from natural commodity money to paper money based on credit, the detrimental impacts of inflation as a form of theft via the state, and the rise of states and the reasons behind their development. We then delved into the concept that statism will ultimately result in complete devastation and conflict until a single state prevails. In order to avert this outcome, we highlighted that there is in fact no requirement for a state to oversee our everyday lives. Society is fully capable of progressing through market forces, which are supported by the ethical foundation of private property. Now, let's examine how we can achieve this goal and either eliminate the state entirely or at the very least, reduce it to an inconsequential presence.

## Cease the Fiat Printer

Anarcho-capitalism may seem appealing, but can it truly alter the world we inhabit? States have already evolved, and the proverbial genie cannot be put back into the lamp. We can, however, counteract the genie by significantly restricting its scope of action through cutting off its financial resources. As previously discussed, advocating for a minimal state is challenging, since the existence of minimal states implies the continuation of states, and in turn, competition between states. This then suggests a state's inclination for expansion via warfare to ensure its survival. Therefore, we cannot argue for a world in which the state is necessary but restrained. Consequently, we must adopt a more radical stance in our argument, stating that while we wish to eradicate the state, we recognize its existence. As such, our goal is to reduce its influence.

It is important to be rational and concede that supplanting the state with anarchy in a single nation is unwise. Even if a solitary nation could forcefully overthrow its government without a new one forming, remaining states would take advantage of the void in power and claim the territory for their gain. While it is theoretically possible for national defense services to be provided through market forces, these defense agencies would not be established quickly enough to deter attacks from other states on our newfound stateless society. All countries across the globe would have to simultaneously overthrow their governments to achieve a stateless world, and the notion of a coordinated worldwide revolution by force can only be deemed preposterous.

An alternative to this irrational global revolution driven by violence is a revolution achieved by detaching states from the production of money, much like separating religion from governance. If we remove the government's ability to create an endless monetary supply via inflation, it would either have to solicit funds (i.e., raise debt) from its constituents for its projects or confront the same decision-making reality as all other economic players. By forcing the government to balance its wants and needs, its capacity to solve problems beyond its original purpose – such as conflict arbitration and private property protection – would be significantly curtailed. Otherwise, it risks losing its legitimacy and ceasing to exist. Consequently, there would be no more government intervention in areas like transportation, education, healthcare, agriculture, research, economy, culture, and energy. Furthermore, any government interference in a market would require the consent of its citizens. If the government desires going to war, it must persuade enough people to support its plans. However, who truly wishes to go to war, apart from the state itself?

But how can we accomplish this monumental task? Why would any government willingly relinquish their seemingly endless source of income created by their magical money printing machines? They would undoubtedly fight to the bitter end to maintain control over such a powerful resource. And exactly who should create our currency? Establishing a network of minters for commodity money coins takes a significant amount of time! How can we transition commodity money into a digital format? It seems implausible to revert back to using physical cash when the entire world is now digital.

These are all legitimate concerns, but there is a single solution that addresses them all: monetary anarchy through the use of Bitcoin. I am aware that some of the readers who have found the arguments presented in this book compelling thus far may be skeptical about this assertion. However, I implore you to approach the following propositions with an open mind, considering them rationally rather than relying on unfounded assumptions (e.g. the notion that Bitcoin's volatility makes it an unsuitable candidate for a monetary asset). Moreover, I would like to clarify that the following discussion is not a dogmatic endorsement of Bitcoin as the one and only viable form of digital currency; rather, it serves to argue in favor of transferring control over money production from the hands of governments to a decentralized system, utilizing an asset with characteristics such as those exhibited by Bitcoin, as a means of preventing financial ruin and perpetual debt for the masses.

As an advocate for free markets, I wholeheartedly encourage competition and welcome any attempts to surpass Bitcoin as the superior monetary asset. However, there are valid reasons to believe that these endeavors will ultimately be fruitless, as the unique nature of Bitcoin's discovery may be impossible to replicate. Much like the momentous discovery of fire, Bitcoin represents a once-in-a-lifetime breakthrough. Could there possibly be a "better" fire? Perhaps, but the idea seems nonsensical. Similarly, searching for a superior form of currency to Bitcoin might be an exercise in futility.

Before delving into why Bitcoin serves as a solution to numerous existing issues, it's important to clarify our aim: to provide a concise explanation of Bitcoin and its significance, focusing on its impact rather than its technical aspects. The vast majority of users (99.9%) will utilize Bitcoin without fully comprehending its inner workings. Thus, understanding the blockchain, Bitcoin mining, or the SHA256 algorithm is not as vital (although there are plenty of excellent books and articles available for those interested in the technical side). What holds far greater importance is the actual value proposition of Bitcoin and its implications for societal change.

It's important to note that even if this book were read by every individual on Earth, it would not be enough to revert back to a commodity-money standard. Not a single thing would change, as the immense effort required to make such a transition would prove too great. As a result, we would continue to tolerate the infringement on our private property through inflation and the existence of the state. Consequently, the only way to combat these forces is by leveraging the power of the market, a process that will inevitably take time. With this in mind, let's explore the true nature of Bitcoin and its significance in the modern era.

# The Ascent of Bitcoin

To assess if you're a proponent of Bitcoin, ask yourself a straightforward question: Must debt be repaid? If you answer affirmatively, then you're a Bitcoiner, even if you don't realize it yet. Believing that debt has value and that such value belongs to someone else, means you believe in property rights. If you accept the notion of property, you also advocate for Bitcoin since it's the purest form of property. Consequently, Bitcoin can be regarded as the embodiment of private property rights, empowering individuals to assert themselves.

What do these private property rights stand for? They function as insurance against irrationality, totalitarianism, enslavement, infringement of speech, corruption, abuse, and most notably, they guarantee a sound night's rest. As the indisputable owner of wealth, you become impervious to corruption, enslavement, and other oppressions. Instead, you gain the freedom to think, become ungovernable, and above all, you develop a critical stance towards anyone who attempts to strip you of your freedom. As a result, Bitcoin represents the ultimate property that protects your autonomy and individuality. Isn't Bitcoin designed to function as a currency? Are we actually exchanging property rights with one another?

Interestingly, this idea is not far from reality, as money essentially represents the exchange of property rights tied to monetary assets. So, what is the underlying monetary asset of Bitcoin? When dealing with commodity money, we know that an item used as currency has an intrinsic market value, apart from its monetary value. After it has been used as currency, both its market and monetary values are considered. For example, the worth of gold coins is the sum of their market value and their monetary value. In contrast, a product without any market value and only monetary value, such as fiat paper currency, would be worth nothing on the free market without legal tender laws. Gold and silver can be used to produce jewelry, and cigarettes can be consumed by smoking, which gives them market value. Bitcoins, however, are just numbers on a screen; they cannot be made into jewelry, and one cannot smoke them. So, where does the market value of Bitcoin originate?

Bitcoin comprises two elements: the payment network and the currency. Both aspects contribute to its value. The simplest way to understand it is that the payment network represents the market value creation, while the currency stands for the monetary value creation. The actual monetary value of Bitcoin will only be uncovered once the market value of its payment network is determined separately. So, what exactly is the market value of the Bitcoin payment network?

The network itself facilitates monetary transactions between parties, allowing individual users to send value via the internet without intermediaries. In other words, conducting transactions on the Bitcoin network turns you into a bank, providing you with the means to save and send value to others in a single unit of account. Saving money and making payments are likely the primary reasons you use banking services in your everyday life. The Bitcoin network can conveniently offer these services without permission from any authority. This simplicity has significant implications: you can transport your net worth anywhere, save money without fearing loss of purchasing power, make small and large global payments, avoid currency exchange fees for foreign transactions, partake in the financial system without government approval, and no one can refuse you financial services.

A significant number of readers may be wondering, "Wait! What are you trying to say? Many of these features already exist and often function more effectively than on the Bitcoin network. For example, Visa and Mastercard handle far more transactions than Bitcoin. So how can something that performs worse than our current system possess any market value?" This is a legitimate concern. The crux of the issue is that the market value of the advantages mentioned above within the Bitcoin payment network does not equate to its actual market value. Rather, the network's market value is symbolized by the option to access all of its advantages without any counterparty risk.

This might seem implausible, but stay with me. What does this mean, and why does an option on something have market value? Remember that Bitcoin serves as insurance. The term "option" in finance is essentially synonymous with "insurance." For instance, imagine you have insurance covering tornado damages to your house for the next five years. If no tornado strikes, or one does but your house remains intact, then your insurance holds no market value after five years. However, if a tornado destroys your home within the next five years, your insurance will cover the costs, and consequently, it has enormous market value. Before the five-year period ends, the insurance policy always retains market value because a tornado might still occur. Thus, as an insurer, you will not provide these policies for free; instead, the insured party must pay a premium to cover the policy.

Accordingly, it's obvious that having an insurance policy has market value, and Bitcoin offers insurance against counterparty risk. Now, let's address why having insurance to transact with one another without taking on counterparty risk represents market value. Suppose you're a stock market investor who invests in a company whose product turns out to be fraudulent. The company goes bankrupt, and the investor loses their money. By purchasing stock in the hope of making a profit, you accept the counterparty risk of the company's default. We can define counterparty risk as the default risk inherent in every financial transaction. When you transact with a dollar or another fiat currency, you implicitly bear the counterparty risk that the government issuing the currency does not go bankrupt, otherwise, your money is worthless. Counterparty risk also involves interference with the financial services you use. If you have saved money with a bank, and the bank collaborates with the government and flags your account for suspicious transactions, the government can order the bank to close your account and seize your assets. This happened, for example, when the US confiscated its citizens' gold holdings in 1933. Gold deposited with banks was turned over to the government without the explicit consent of the bank's clients, so by using the banks' custody services, the clients accepted the counterparty risk.

Bitcoin eliminates counterparty risk because the Bitcoin network is a peer-to-peer network that doesn't require any financial intermediaries. Thus, when we transact on the Bitcoin network, we deal directly with each other as if exchanging cash, and no middleman is present that could jeopardize our transactions in any way. We also don't have to worry about anyone changing the rules governing the Bitcoin network, as it operates based on computer code that is publicly visible to everyone. Consequently, every network participant is protected from any alterations to these rules. As a Bitcoin holder, you know what you're getting, and you don't need to worry about third-party interference since no central authority could make such changes. The moment you lose trust in the financial system you're currently using, the Bitcoin payment network becomes incredibly valuable because you don't need anyone's permission to create a Bitcoin address and start transacting. Therefore, the market value of the Bitcoin payment network originates from the option value of transacting with other parties without any counterparty risk. No one can take your Bitcoins away if they don't have the private key to your wallet, which is a software or application that holds and safeguards your Bitcoin holdings.

Expanding on the market value of the Bitcoin payment network, we can now explore the monetary value that Bitcoin as a currency embodies. We established that for an item to serve as money, it must be the ideal medium of exchange and have the highest marketability. The criteria applied include durability, portability, divisibility, fungibility, scarcity, and acceptability. Bitcoin as a currency is the most marketable good in the Bitcoin payment network, as it is the only currency the network accepts for initiating transactions. Moreover, Bitcoin as a currency comes closest to humanity's discovery of the perfect good to use as a monetary asset.

Bitcoin the currency is perfectly scarce, with an unchangeable fixed supply of 21 million Bitcoins. There will never be more Bitcoins than that. Additionally, as a digital asset, Bitcoin is perfectly durable and fungible. Every Bitcoin is identical, and there are no different classifications of Bitcoins. The characteristics with the most significant societal impact, besides scarcity, are Bitcoin's infinite divisibility and high portability. Bitcoin can be repeatedly split into smaller units called Sats. Therefore, regardless of the economy's growth, Bitcoin can always accommodate the appropriate prices for all goods in the marketplace. Additionally, the simple portability of Bitcoin allows for nimble capital movement. It cannot be trapped in regulations, laws, or violence, and it can be sent anywhere with a single click.

There has never been a better good to qualify as sound money than Bitcoin. As a result, Bitcoin as a concept (including the Bitcoin payment network and the Bitcoin currency) holds tremendous value and is the best money ever created because it has market value due to its payment network and monetary value due to its currency.

The average person may not construct such a detailed argument to decide why they should use Bitcoin as money over any other good. The market will play its part and educate market participants over time, whether through painful experiences (financial crises, inflation, etc.) or incentives (cheaper and more efficient use of financial services than in our current financial system). Consequently, humanity doesn't need to understand Bitcoin's value creation process, as its value is demonstrated by real-world use cases, such as sending money from the US to African countries without incurring the exorbitant fees that financial intermediaries impose on such transactions.

In conclusion, the value of each Bitcoin symbolizes the option value of having access to a financial system free from corruption, coercion, and centralization. The more humanity faces oppression from governments, the stronger the desire for freedom. Consequently, as the world becomes increasingly tyrannical, the value of Bitcoin will only increase.

## The Adoption of Bitcoin

Although Bitcoin is undoubtedly a superior financial asset compared to any fiat currency, it cannot logically persuade the world to adopt it. Simply informing every person on the planet about Bitcoin will not change their habits until it becomes a necessity. As humans, we have an inherent tendency to be lazy, only taking action when we must or when there is a clear advantage to doing so. As a result, people must experience the hardships of being unbanked, facing limited access to financial services, or losing their purchasing power due to inflation before considering an alternative financial system. However, once this transition occurs, there is no turning back.

Bitcoin's adoption is currently hindered by its technical usage, which requires individuals to have substantial financial literacy. Unfortunately, the people who need it most, mainly those living in impoverished areas of the Global South, are often the least educated. Therefore, Bitcoin must bridge the educational gap and, most importantly, raise awareness of its existence among the economically disadvantaged. It's understandable that individuals with limited financial resources may be skeptical of new financial technologies, primarily because they have only experienced exploitation by the wealthy through financial policies. In this context, Bitcoin's claim of being "magic internet money" may not be particularly appealing when one's survival depends on affording basic necessities. In the North and Western hemispheres, access to basic banking services is generally easier, and the effect of inflation is less severe than for those using less stable currencies. Consequently, the demand for an alternative is not as crucial for these individuals. However, this perspective can quickly shift when governments overreach and interfere with citizens' privacy and financial activities. The more financially challenged a person is, the easier it is for them to transition to Bitcoin. This situation creates a unique opportunity for the financially oppressed to benefit from embracing a new financial order before those with greater wealth.

At first glance, it might appear that not only ordinary citizens but also governments that are currently subjected to dollar hegemony or opposed to US foreign policy would have strong motives to adopt Bitcoin as their primary financial asset. Under the current global financial system, the US dollar is the reserve currency, giving the American central bank and the US government exclusive power to print more dollars. This authority grants the US government unparalleled control over the global money supply. Ideally, governments would prefer controlling their own financial systems without being accountable to others. However, if this is not feasible, it may be more advantageous to operate under a decentralized currency's financial framework with fixed rules than to be beholden to another government with divergent interests. Regrettably, this is not the prevailing sentiment. While governments resent their financial dependence on the US for international transactions, they reject the idea of a world where they lack control over their own currency's money supply even more. As a result, states and their central banks will likely be the final entities to embrace Bitcoin and monetary anarchy as a financial standard. This is because Bitcoin aims to address the flaws within the existing financial system and establish a strong, non-manipulatable monetary foundation for the world.

The remaining question is whether Bitcoin's adoption will be a peaceful process or if governments around the world will wage war on individual freedom and self-determination, descending into authoritarian rule. If history serves as any guide, it's evident that governments will go to any lengths to ensure their survival, leaving no option off-limits. Consequently, the path to Bitcoin's global acceptance must be a gradual, bottom-up approach, persuading one person at a time to become a Bitcoin supporter until the world can no longer dismiss it as a criminal tool. At that point, the facade of democracy behind which governments conceal themselves may finally crumble, exposing the harsh reality of corruption, manipulation, power-hunger, oppression, and dictatorship. Hopefully, this revelation will transpire because once a government's true nature is unveiled, it forfeits all legitimacy and collapses like a house of cards. Eventually, Bitcoin will triumph, steering humanity away from its current destructive course. The only uncertainty is when and how tumultuous the journey will become before improving.

## Can Bitcoin be Prevented?

Before exploring the possible attack vectors that Bitcoin could be vulnerable to, let's examine the psychological reasons that make Bitcoin the most significant digital cryptocurrency. After all, a substantial portion of the financial system relies on psychology. Technically, Bitcoin could be replicated, as its code is publicly accessible to everyone. Anyone can obtain the code, modify it, and create a new cryptocurrency. The market then determines if the altered version is superior to the original. However, what distinguishes Bitcoin and renders it unique is its leaderless, anonymous nature, and most importantly, its status as an idea or even an ideal, rather than merely computer code.

Firstly, Bitcoin operates as an open-source project with no central authority, rendering it the only completely decentralized cryptocurrency. All other cryptocurrencies are centralized and can be manipulated by their creators, similar to how fiat currencies can be interfered with by the governments that issue them. Bitcoin's creator, Satoshi Nakamoto, disappeared following its inception and has never reappeared. It is unknown whether Bitcoin was created by an individual, a group, a woman, or a man. Nonetheless, it can be asserted with certainty that the creator is no longer involved, as the Bitcoins in the original wallet are no longer in circulation, and the creator would have forgone enormous wealth by not redeeming their Bitcoin, which is highly improbable. If the creator were to be revealed, it could potentially alter Bitcoin's mechanics, as the assumption of no counterparty risk is based on the fact that no single entity controls Bitcoin. As it stands, Bitcoin remains free from individual interference and serves as an impartial platform for global monetary transactions in cyberspace. It is difficult to envision that any future cryptocurrency could replicate this same neutrality due to the absence of anonymity among its creators. Even if a cryptocurrency were to achieve this, it would also need to endure the passage of time. This process cannot be accelerated - founders cannot vanish for a year and claim that their currency is as founderless as Bitcoin. Since time cannot be rewound, Bitcoin will always be the cryptocurrency with the longest history of its creators' absence, making it impossible to surpass in terms of neutrality.

Secondly, just as fire can only be discovered once, it is impossible to rediscover fire. If we did, we would instantly recognize it as fire and understand its value. When Bitcoin was introduced to the world, no one comprehended what it was. As a result, it could develop its following organically, without being influenced by monetary incentives. In contrast, every other cryptocurrency is immediately recognized as such and attracts speculators and investors who, once the hype surrounding the current one fades, migrate to the next popular cryptocurrency. Consequently, Bitcoin's diehard supporters could flourish under non-economic conditions, as they are idealists rather than opportunists. It is practically impossible for another cryptocurrency to replicate this fertile environment. Due to Bitcoin's previous success, no other digital currency can be created under the same conditions that allowed Bitcoin to prosper initially. If something else proves to be a superior form of money, it cannot be a blockchain-based digital cryptocurrency but must take an entirely different form.

So the real question that Bitcoin's critics must ask themselves is: how can they destroy an idea? It is true that knowledge has vanished over the centuries, but Bitcoin has already permeated every corner of the world, making it impossible to eradicate the concept of decentralized, censorship-resistant money from the collective human consciousness. So if they cannot eliminate it, can they at least discourage its use?

Ultimately, Bitcoin can be attacked through technical, political, or financial means. Technically, the Bitcoin network can be hacked, its hardware compromised, or access to the internet infrastructure on which it depends can be denied to its users. Indeed, it cannot be ruled out that there may be technical flaws in the computer code that Bitcoin employs, nor can it be denied that hackers might discover a vulnerability to exploit the Bitcoin network at any given moment. We also cannot discount the possibility that a super quantum computer or artificial intelligence algorithm will emerge in the future, surpassing anything humanity has ever witnessed, which would be capable of infiltrating, altering, or destroying the Bitcoin network. However, we can assert with confidence that Bitcoin represents the largest honeypot of monetary value ever created. Hacking Bitcoin would instantly make one the wealthiest person in the world. Using the analogy of a bank heist, hackers have attempted to rob the Bitcoin bank since its inception but have failed repeatedly. Consequently, Bitcoin has the longest record of being impervious to compromise among digital currencies.

Governments might attempt to collaborate with one another to force computer hardware and chip manufacturers to install malware on their devices, which can be used to spy on Bitcoin users or exploit them in other ways. Since tech-savvy users safeguarding the Bitcoin network are likely to detect such attacks relatively quickly, affected manufacturers would be replaced by emerging competitors. Thus, while governments may temporarily confuse users and undermine trust in the Bitcoin network, it will ultimately emerge stronger. Additionally, governments can limit internet access, as seen in China, or completely shut down the internet to eradicate Bitcoin. It is my sincere hope that "shutting down the internet" sounds as absurd to you as it does to me, and something only a foolish economist would propose. Similar to the internet, Bitcoin is a network based on millions of computers and devices worldwide. If one country shuts down its internet and telecommunications services, the Bitcoin network continues to operate everywhere else as usual, with the affected country regaining access once they are back online. If every country on the planet simultaneously shut down the internet, other dire consequences would arise, as our global economy, healthcare system, and national security all rely on the internet and computer networks. Only an apocalyptic event can prompt such a scenario, making Bitcoin irrelevant if no one remains to use it.

More threatening than technical failures are political attacks. Governments might employ any tool in their propaganda arsenal to declare Bitcoin an enemy of humanity. Keep in mind that statism and governmental authority are fueled by propaganda and ideology, convincing us that property theft through taxes and inflation is justifiable. As a result, governments are adept at crafting narratives, persuading their constituents that they act in their best interests. Thus, the political propaganda attack vector poses a genuine threat. If governments convince people that Bitcoin is environmentally damaging and only used by criminals for human trafficking or by terrorists to fund attacks, the average person may question its legitimacy. We can only encourage you to critically examine every argument posed by Bitcoin detractors. For example, consider the myth that Bitcoin is harmful to the environment because the proof-of-work mechanism securing the network consumes vast amounts of electricity, primarily produced by burning fossil fuels, which then impact the climate. Although such a contention might convince our uninformed elders that their descendants resemble the devil, take into account the following: Bitcoin mining companies, like any other economic participants, are motivated by profits. They strive to carry out their operations as economically efficient as possible, searching for the least costly electricity source. Interestingly, the most affordable electricity comes from solar power. As a result, Bitcoin miners dependent on fossil fuel-based electricity will lose out to those employing solar energy. This implies that Bitcoin actually opposes government assertions by advocating for the use of renewable energy sources and discouraging "dirty" electricity. I cannot possibly refute all the propaganda assaults Bitcoin has been subjected to, but I strongly encourage you to examine beyond the surface and form your own opinions.

Ironically, by adhering to sound financial practices and advocating individual freedom, governments hold the key to either significantly delaying Bitcoin adoption or strongly dissuading its use in the first place. People have far less motivation to use an alternative financial system if they are not oppressed, stripped of their individual freedom rights, and do not fear their purchasing power eroding, particularly because using the Bitcoin network remains relatively technical compared to traditional fiat systems. However, doing so requires the state to surrender the power it has fiercely acquired back to its constituents. Since states constantly worry about their survival both internally and externally, relinquishing any power accumulated over time is highly counterintuitive and contrary to the nature of statism. Therefore, even though the attack vector of fiscal restraint by governments might actually be the only genuine short-term threat to Bitcoin, in the long run (and I truly mean the long run, think 100-200 years plus), the best currency will prevail. Consequently, Bitcoin may be hindered by financial integrity, but it is ultimately unstoppable.

It is vital to comprehend that Bitcoin exemplifies an antifragile asset. Antifragility implies that something becomes more robust when exposed to shocks and stressors rather than weaker. Picture Bitcoin as a hydra from Greek mythology battling a swordsman. Each time the swordsman cuts off one of the hydra's heads, two more grow back, making the creature even stronger. This principle applies to Bitcoin. Whenever it weathers an attack from any vector and survives, users' faith in Bitcoin's resilience improves.

Since its inception, critics have proclaimed Bitcoin dead daily, and it has withstood countless attacks from hackers, governments, and adversaries. The recurring lesson is that the Bitcoin network remains impervious at a technical level and has never stopped functioning. Although exploiting the financial vector may be the government's most effective approach, it is highly unlikely they will attack Bitcoin in this manner, as it involves curbing their money printing activities and managing their spending. Historically, governments' primary objective has been to expand and consolidate their power, leading to incessant conflict with other governments. As such, they cannot financially restrain themselves.

As a result, governments will utilize their political toolbox, including propaganda and the spread of false narratives, in an attempt to counteract the rise of Bitcoin. Be prepared for potential accusations of being a climate terrorist or child abuser if you use Bitcoin, but also recognize that the more aggressively governments attack Bitcoin, the closer we are to its widespread adoption.

# Monetary Anarchy

The adoption of the Bitcoin monetary standard will greatly impact society as a whole and the operation of the financial system. Before proceeding, I would like to emphasize that I will not delve into the intricacies of making the Bitcoin network functional for millions of smaller transactions in our everyday lives (scaling through the Lightning network) or how to authenticate users on the blockchain (digital passports for establishing credit scores) to facilitate loans and credit. While these are critical concerns, the technical obstacles will be overcome in due course. As we have seen in a previous chapter, the market is entirely capable of supplying any commodity it genuinely requires. Admittedly, the market may occasionally need to take a roundabout route to acquire what it seeks, but it ultimately obtains the desired products. Therefore I will rather shine a light on the consequences Bitcoin will bring to money and banking, the shift in logic of the organization of violence in the form of the state and the implications for economic productivity.

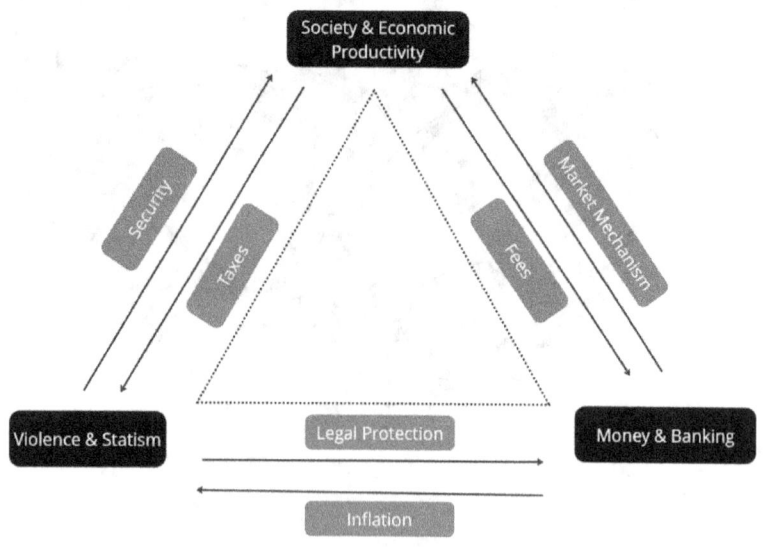

*Societal organization before the rise of monetary anarchy through Bitcoin*

Before Bitcoin came into existence, human society was structured around the fundamental principles of three pillars: productivity, collaboration, and violence. These concepts may be referred to by different names across various academic fields, but their core significance remains unchanged. Productivity represents human endeavor and economic productivity, while cooperation encompasses the market mechanism (division of labor) through money or other means of exchange. Violence takes the form of a government, state, or any authority with a local monopoly on the use of force. In an ideal anarcho-capitalist society, individuals adhere to the non-aggression principle, enabling them to produce and trade without the presence of violence. Although it may be theoretically possible for a market system to support such arrangements, history has shown that human emotions get in the way of economic reason.

The state, with its local monopoly on violence, has primarily evolved into the mediator of conflicts. However, it has abused its societal role to corrupt the financial system and, consequently, the market mechanism for collaboration. By monopolizing the money market and implementing legal tender regulations to safeguard the banking industry, the government has successfully managed to secure a source of revenue through inflation by exploiting its power over force. This inflationary process results in unidentified victims, without affecting the state's credibility.

The banking sector embraced the arrangement, as it enabled them to prosper due to their close association with the state. The agreement's only victims are the workers who produce the wealth that the state and banks eagerly extract. Ultimately, society settles for inadequate protection from violence in exchange for excessive taxation and a financial system that deprives them of their hard-earned rewards. The world we live in is a travesty of any society that genuinely values hard work and economic production. It is no longer acceptable for humanity to support a social structure where productivity is deterred, and lethargy, parasitism, immorality, and misguided calls for equality guide our species' trajectory.

Unfortunately, due to the limitations of commodity money, we failed to avoid the grim reality we currently face. The rise of fiat money coincides with human advancement and capitalizes on our vulnerabilities as a species. Indeed, fiat money had its advantages and served as an effective means of expanding the money supply when humanity needed it most. Our conquest of nature and the world would have progressed at a far slower pace if not for the rapid coordination enabled by fiat money. However, the restrictive nature of physical money is no longer relevant with the introduction of the Bitcoin monetary standard. Consequently, fiat money has outlived its usefulness. In fact, its ample quantity and vulnerability to manipulation have turned it into a favored tool for a select elite that controls the world. It is time to liberate ourselves from the bonds that have turned humanity into its current, flawed state and rekindle the appreciation for hard work and productivity with the help of monetary anarchy as an unyielding force that champions humanity while resisting oppression.

# The Rehabilitation of Money

After reading this book, you understand that money serves as an invisible network, linking and coordinating all human actions. Prices indicate to the market how valuable a product is, the necessary supply of that product, and when a product is no longer required. When governments interfere with the money supply, they hinder human coordination, resulting in resource misallocation due to government intervention. As a result, determining the proper size of our money supply, establishing rules for its modification or maintenance, and deciding who has the authority to do so are critical aspects of the human experience. When a select few gain control over our money supply while the majority passively submit to their fate, our world devolves into a system of debt enslavement.

The emergence of Bitcoin indicates a major shift in the world of money production. The Bitcoin network will reintroduce fairness and justice into the financial system, ensuring that each participant receives what they truly deserve. Bitcoin has the potential to alleviate financial disparities and reduce financial cronyism among humanity. It is important to note that the gap between the wealthy and the less fortunate may still exist or even widen in the short term under a Bitcoin standard, primarily due to the prevalence of poor financial decision-making. Equality, in this context, refers to equal access to financial systems and their functions. The responsibility for using these systems falls on the individual, rather than Bitcoin itself. As such, Bitcoin will facilitate the transition from an insider-driven Ponzi economy to a neutral platform for coordination. Money should never serve as a tool for manipulation or social engineering but should instead aid all market participants in directing their efforts where they are most required, adhering to publicly available rules. Your earning, saving, and spending abilities will no longer be determined by the political system in place.

With a limited supply of 21 million Bitcoins, our inflationary, debt-based financial system can be revolutionized and transformed into a deflationary, equity-based economy. By acquiring Bitcoin, you can protect your assets from inflation, unlike with traditional fiat currency. Instead of having an expiration date like conventional money, the value of Bitcoin will likely increase over time. Why? As the economy grows and generates more goods and services, the fixed supply of 21 million Bitcoin remains constant, causing prices to decrease. This incentivizes those who practice financial prudence and penalizes those who live beyond their means. Establishing a dependable commodity money system was not possible in the past due to the difficulty of dividing commodities, which made it challenging to maintain a stable monetary foundation for all economic activities. However, Bitcoin's capability to be infinitely divided into smaller units enables the creation of a deflationary monetary system.

However, haven't prominent economists and politicians warned us about the risks of falling prices? Yes, they have. But this argument primarily favors those who misuse their authority to generate fiat currency, benefiting from inflation without comprehending the notion of saving. In our current financial system, money can be created with a simple click of a computer button. When a banker issues a loan, they generate money out of thin air without having saved it beforehand. This allows them to lend money essentially to whoever they believe can repay it, without risking their existing assets (though this is an oversimplification, it is generally accurate). If a bank can only extend credit based on its previous earnings, it will be more cautious in its lending practices. As a result, debt will only be pursued when necessary and only by those capable of repaying it.

Some critics may assert that credit is fundamental to human development and that restricting access to it will hinder progress. While this argument has merit, it is essential to consider the broader implications of credit. Essentially, credit serves as a bet on a brighter future, in which you borrow from your future self to afford something in the present. This can be a fantastic opportunity when investing in yourself or a business, but it can also lead to poor financial decisions when used for consumption. By limiting credit options, individuals must save capital to afford a desired good, which requires time. Consequently, human progress may be delayed since capital must be saved before embarking on projects that improve the world. However, this may not be a negative outcome.

Firstly, limiting access to capital allows us to concentrate on the most urgent and significant challenges. Instead of focusing on unnecessary projects made possible through excessive debt, we can prioritize those that drive humanity forward. Secondly, the process of accumulating capital is a vital aspect of any financial journey, as it enables the market to adapt to new realities. We are in a period where critical technologies, such as quantum computing, artificial intelligence, and bioinformatics, are at a tipping point, poised to experience exponential growth and have a lasting impact on humanity. Reflecting on the vast history of humankind, how significant are the 30 years it might take, for example, to amass the necessary capital to initiate a significant project in one of those fields? Not much. However, rushing into decisions leads to irreversible consequences, and some effects only become apparent over time.

To make this argument more applicable to our everyday lives, let's think about the time that inflation and the constant need to maintain our financial status has taken away from our relationships with family and friends. Establishing financial discipline through limiting credit will ultimately prove advantageous for humankind, freeing us from irrationality and misguided desires. It is vital that we face the consequences of our actions, recognizing that we do not inhabit a world of boundless resources but one of scarcity. Our monetary system should represent this reality by imposing choices upon humanity. It is important to clarify that my argument does not praise Luddites who oppose technological advancements. Instead, I champion technology as a crucial tool in humanity's continuous struggle against nature. Nevertheless, we must ensure that our progress does not lead to a dystopian future dominated by a small ruling class with exclusive access to the monetary system's benefits, governing a legion of debt-ridden individuals.

Transitioning to the deflationary Bitcoin standard will present challenges. With money becoming more valuable over time, repaying acquired debt will be increasingly difficult. This mathematical truth will precipitate the collapse of the unstable structure erected over the past century, resulting in debt liquidations, government and corporate defaults. This economic distress will impact many, and lives may be lost. It is essential to understand that the hardships following the introduction of the Bitcoin standard cannot be blamed on Bitcoin itself. As mentioned before, Bitcoin is a neutral platform governed by apolitical mathematical rules. The consequences of the fiat system's collapse can only be ascribed to governments and banks worldwide that have held the free world captive for far too long. From the remnants of financial chaos, Bitcoin will rise as a new, impartial, and neutral monetary standard upon which humanity can construct its future.

This future will be prosperous because it relies on a firm foundation and encourages responsible financial habits by merely returning money's ability to serve as a tool for savings and capital preservation. In an inflationary economy, capital cannot accumulate in cash or money reserves as the money supply's increase diminishes its value. Consequently, money must be invested in assets like real estate, stocks, or other goods like art, which increase in value as the money supply expands. Regrettably, most people lack access to assets as they are used for savings and their prohibitive costs prevent ownership. In a deflationary environment, however, money can buy more goods over time, fulfilling its original purpose of protecting capital and serving as an ideal savings vehicle. Asset prices will be more affordable tomorrow, making them accessible to anyone willing to forgo immediate desires for future goals. Consequently, all assets currently functioning as savings vehicles, such as real estate, will be "demonetized" and valued based on their societal function rather than their ability to preserve capital.

Financial crises, business cycles, and liquidity crunches will eventually vanish as they stem from an inflationary fiat money system. The fundamental principle that one can only spend what one earns will shield us from unnecessary economic struggles and the immorality of socializing financial mismanagement. Banks will need to embrace their primary societal role as money creators and custody service providers. Though it would be ideal, it is unlikely that Bitcoin will be widely used by most individuals in the near future due to its technical nature. As a result, banks or other financial entrepreneurs will bridge the gap by offering their own user-friendly currencies backed by Bitcoin and providing custody services akin to those of commodity money warehouses and minters. The crucial differences will be that banks will find it difficult to lend money in a deflationary environment, and states and governments will no longer be able to rescue them in cases of financial mismanagement. Users will, therefore, learn through experience who can be trusted and who cannot.

In conclusion, the future of humanity will see money and finance playing a less significant role than at present. Money should not be a daily concern or something we need to monitor constantly to avoid being deceived. Instead, it should serve as a neutral instrument to facilitate human cooperation in our productive endeavors. With the Bitcoin monetary platform, we have the capacity to achieve monetary anarchy - the separation of money production from the state - and bring about profoundly positive implications for our species as a whole.

# Wealth by Merit, not Circumstance

Society as a whole is centered on economic productivity, with the action axiom revealing that human action is necessary for survival. These actions together form the global economy, the core of human existence. The mistreatment of property rights throughout history and the manipulation by an elite group to exploit economic value from actual producers is appalling. It is astonishing that modern society seeks exploitation under the guise of equality, being unable to link individual challenges, such as housing or education affordability, to the negative effects of government overreach. Though the public realizes the system is unfair, they struggle to pinpoint the mechanisms, pushing for simplistic solutions like equality and fairness instead. This has led to a surge in socialism, seen as a simple answer to a complex problem. However, the problem lies in the contradiction between fairness and equality when applied to humans. The redistribution of resources from one individual to another in the name of equality tends to unfairly disadvantage at least one party involved.

The introduction of the Bitcoin standard offers a more equitable opportunity for all to achieve economic goals based on a morally defensible private property framework, rather than equal outcomes. Since human action relies on self-ownership, it is neither desirable nor morally valid for individuals to have identical results. Individualism should be the principal motivator for any action. Bitcoin levels the playing field in financial matters, eliminating special treatment for the politically connected and removing safety nets for irresponsible economic actors. Consequences must be faced for excessive risk-taking, with no expectation of humanity bailing anyone out.

But what occurs when banks and governments believe they can continue their unethical practices of taking excessive risks on their balance sheets? What if they consistently make poor business decisions and fail to recover funds from borrowers? The simple answer is bankruptcy. The nuanced distinction between a debt- and equity-based financial system is that in an equity-based system, there is no bailout if poor decisions lead to excessive risk-taking. Gone are the days of government bailouts as a safety net for unscrupulous bankers and mismanaged corporations. This also applies to sovereign powers and governments. If a government overspends and cannot repay its debt, it defaults as it cannot print money to resolve its problems. Consequently, governments refocus on their core competencies, such as law enforcement and national security.

Bankruptcies may seem negative, but they are a natural part of the economy. By repeatedly bailing out companies without a genuine need for their services, we risk creating a stagnant economy that blocks new ventures from emerging. When business decisions become politicized and winners are selected based on favors rather than merit, society deteriorates from within. The idea of bankruptcy prevents those who are currently successful from dominating in the future, ensuring that everyone has an equal chance to succeed. This means that generational wealth is not guaranteed, promoting a true meritocracy. Even if parents are wealthy, their children are not entitled to their wealth, and making poor financial decisions can lead to losing that wealth.

Understanding inequality as a potentially positive market outcome, rather than an inherent negative, is crucial. Inequality could change at any given moment as a result of market processes. The social order that develops under a Bitcoin standard is dynamic and resistant to political influence and control. Bitcoin rewards competence and skill while punishing laziness and wastefulness. Upward mobility will be as prevalent as downward mobility. In essence, the Bitcoin monetary standard acts as a leveling force for social status, ensuring today's wealthy must continue to provide value to the market to remain affluent in the future.

## States as Service Providers

Throughout history, transformative changes have often occurred when there was a shift in the logic of violence. These shifts can be attributed to the direct influence of improved weaponry (from wood to metal, gunpowder, atomic bomb), or due to the indirect impact of expanding knowledge among the masses, bringing about revolution (such as the printing press and the subsequent decline of the church). The emergence of Bitcoin as a new monetary standard will not be exempt from this rule, as it directly influences the logic of violence.

Bitcoin will transfer monetary value to cyberspace, enabling market participants to conduct transactions beyond government-imposed financial systems. Consequently, governments will endure substantial difficulties in capturing a portion of this value as the return on investment for employing violence against cyberspace players dwindles dramatically. When market participants reside within a single physical location, it is comparatively more manageable for the government to seize value in the form of taxes and through physical coercion. However, with the value arising from digital productivity, the situation shifts. Governments must go to extreme lengths to seize a part of that value, resulting in the ROI on applying violence rapidly diminishing. This process is already underway and can be seen in the open seas and the North and South Poles. No one claims these territories, as the return on investment (ROI) for aggression is insufficient. Therefore, freedom reigns supreme, and cyberspace can be compared to a larger version of Antarctica. To maintain their standing within the Bitcoin monetary framework, governments need to adapt their value propositions.

Governments need to recognize that they cannot exploit their citizens without facing consequences. They should stop seeing themselves as aggressive expansionists who exploit their constituents for productivity, and instead, see themselves as providers of security and arbitration services for the market. If they attempt to expand beyond that scope, they risk disqualification and being deemed illegitimate.

Yet, the current reality is that the quality of government services is declining globally, and costs continue to rise. With the Bitcoin standard, capital will be more mobile and available 24/7 worldwide. As a result, states will be subject to the same market forces and intense competition among jurisdictions as corporations. The internet has already shown the fate of economically friendly and unfriendly jurisdictions. Countries like Singapore, Cyprus, Malta, and the UAE have proven that low taxes, freedom, and individuality lead to economic growth. If their value proposition for constituent services is lacking, people will simply switch allegiances to another state. Consequently, states will no longer have subjects to rule over. Instead, they must treat their constituents as customers, as it will become easier for individuals to move between countries with their economic value. While there has never been a precedent for severely limiting states, adopting Bitcoin makes this scenario increasingly plausible.

This circumstance primarily benefits highly productive citizens who contribute significantly to tax revenue. The implication is that oppressive states will mainly affect the poor, who cannot escape their circumstances. This issue is further worsened for the poor as the state struggles to redistribute wealth to the unproductive due to their limited income. Consequently, the welfare state's best days have passed, and the future will be built on individuality rather than socialistic illusions.

It is evident that states will initially exert significant effort to stop the exodus of productivity from their territories, resorting to outdated methods such as holding productive individuals' relatives hostage and demanding ransom. They will show extreme hostility to those trying to evade their grasp and deter others by making an example of them. Laws and force will restrict access to Bitcoin. Bitcoin wallet manufacturers will face bans, Bitcoin mining will be prohibited, information will be disrupted and censored, and services assisting individuals in switching countries will be scrutinized through propaganda and public shame. In the final transitional phase, our reality will resemble the Big Brother surveillance found in dystopian science fiction novels. However, the darkest hours come before dawn, and eventually, centralized governments will recognize that democracy and statism, in their current forms, are incompatible with the information age and the Bitcoin monetary standard. Similar to how the Holy Church currently provides spiritual sanctuary, states will exist in relative obscurity, except for the security services they offer.

## The Separation of Money and State

We have made significant progress in comprehending the true nature of money and the ways in which its production has been monopolized by the government. My aim has been to elucidate the reasons behind the emergence of states and to argue that their existence cannot be justified on either moral or practical grounds. Instead, I have endeavored to show that the very existence of states poses a danger to humanity, pushing us towards chaos and conflict. It is my hope that I have effectively conveyed the significance of Bitcoin, not only in terms of individual financial advantage, but by situating it within the larger framework of economic and political thought.

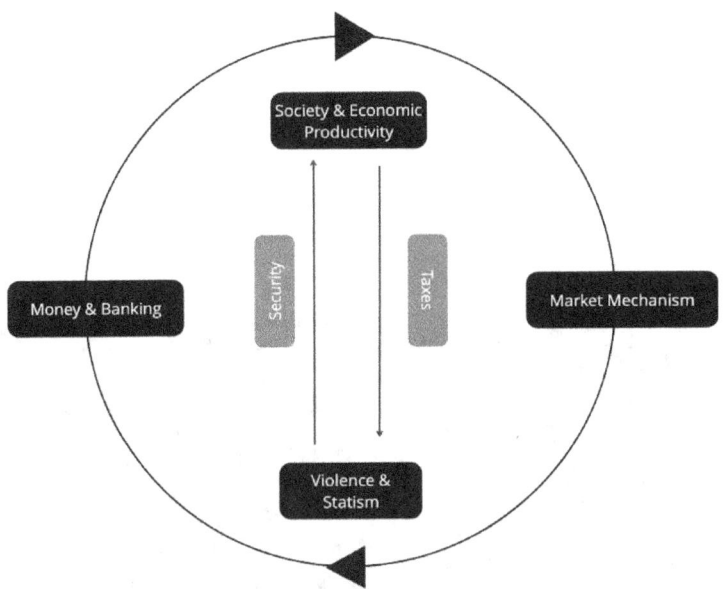

*The Bitcoin platform of monetary value*

I sincerely hope that you will ultimately determine that detaching our financial system and the process of creating money from government control is beneficial to society. Admittedly, considering the potential changes the world may undergo and envisioning the possible future can be daunting. However, this hesitancy to accept change should not justify the maintenance of the status quo. Nations exist in a state of anarchy, striving to outdo one another, which will result in the devastation of war. To prevent this outcome, we must encourage the widespread adoption of Bitcoin as a platform for monetary independence - a neutral space that severs ties to governments, the banking system, and the shortcomings of human nature, while promoting self-reliance, private property rights, virtue, diligence, merit, and technological deflationary aspects. Government control over our money is not necessary for human progress. Instead, the market mechanism will consistently discover superior solutions when compared to any government intervention. Bitcoin exemplifies the ultimate monetary asset, offering the first opportunity in history to create such a neutral financial platform. Let us seize this opportunity and not let it go to waste.

# Closing Remarks

The main message to extract from this book emphasizes the significance of independent thinking and raising challenging questions, even when the answers might be disconcerting. In the opening section, I endeavored to clarify the differences between "a priori" and "a posteriori" understanding. My earnest desire is for you not to validate any hypotheses presented in this book through observation immediately. Instead, your focus should be on understanding the significance and consequences of Bitcoin as a neutral monetary system.

Governments across the globe seek to divert their citizens' attention, convincing them that the political spectrum is confined to left-wing and right-wing ideologies, thereby obscuring the genuine struggle between personal autonomy and central authority from public perception. I understand the allure of overlooking this truth, but I urge you to refrain from doing so.

Take charge of your destiny and liberate yourself from the prevailing narrative. Embark on an independent intellectual journey. No single book can encompass the entirety of the world's wisdom. Hence, I have chosen not to attempt to incorporate all the details you need to thoroughly understand Bitcoin and its consequences. Instead, my aim was to offer thoughts that will hopefully encourage you to examine unsettling questions, recognizing that traditional sources provide only traditional knowledge. Don't be afraid to break away from the boundaries of conformity. While the less-traveled path may be tough, choosing independence and freedom may be better than being trapped as a prisoner of convention.

When you choose to support Bitcoin, keep in mind that this decision is for the benefit of future generations rather than just yourself. However, achieving freedom through Bitcoin comes at a price and requires persistent effort. You must recognize that the journey will be tough and relentless. Reading this book alone will not suffice; you should delve into other resources such as books, videos, podcasts, and articles to expand your understanding of financial history and Bitcoin intricacies. Additionally, you should educate your loved ones about Bitcoin. Although Bitcoin itself doesn't oblige you to do anything, humanity does - it urges you to advocate for liberty and emancipation from fiat currency. You can participate in this battle by spreading awareness about Bitcoin, which will contribute more than you might expect.

The best days of humanity lie ahead, not in the past. Let us march toward a bright, orange future and never look back.

## Vires in numeris

# Bibliography & Acknowledgements

We all rely on the contributions of intellectual titans, and without these references, "Monetary Anarchy: The Separation of Money and State" would not have been possible.

## Books

[1] *Ammous, Saifedean*. **The Bitcoin Standard**. Wiley, 2018.

[2] *Ammous, Saifedean*. **The Fiat Standard**. The Saif House, 2021.

[3] *Antonopoulos, Andreas*. **The Internet of Money, Volume I**. Merkle Bloom LLC, 2016.

[4] *Antonopoulos, Andreas*. **The Internet of Money, Volume II**. Merkle Bloom LLC, 2017.

[5] *Antonopoulos, Andreas*. **The Internet of Money, Volume III**. Merkle Bloom LLC, 2019.

[6] *Bhatia, Nick*. **Layered Money**. 2021.

[7] *Booth, Jeff*. **The Price of Tomorrow**. Stanley Press, 2020.

[8] *Davidson, James Dale & Lord William Rees-Mogg*. **The Sovereign Individual**. Touchstone, 1999.

[9] Friedman, David. **The Machinery of Freedom**. Writers Representatives LLC, 2014.

[10] *Hayek, Friedrich August*. **The Road to Serfdom**. The University of Chicago Press, 2007.

[11] *Hoppe, Hans-Hermann*. **A Theory of Socialism and Capitalism**. Ludwig von Mises Institute, 2010.

[12] *Hoppe, Hans-Hermann*. **Economy, Society & History**. Ludwig von Mises Institute, 2021.

[13] *Hoppe, Hans-Hermann*. **From Aristocracy to Monarchy to Democracy**. Ludwig von Mises Institute, 2014.

[14] *Hoppe, Hans-Hermann*. **The Economics and Ethics of Private Property**. Ludwig von Mises Institute, 2006.

[15] *Hudson, Michael*. **Super Imperialism**. Islet, 2021.

[16] *Hudson, Michael*. **The Destiny of Civilization**. Islet, 2022.

[17] *Hülsmann, Jörg Guido*. **Deflation and Liberty**. Ludwig von Mises Institute, 2008.

[18] *Hülsmann, Jörg Guido.* **The Ethics of Money Production.** Ludwig von Mises Institute, 2008.

[19] *Nozick, Robert.* **Anarchy, State, and Utopia.** Basic Books, 2013.

[20] *Rawls, John.* **A Theory of Justice.** Harvard College, 1971.

[21] *Rothbard, Murray.* **For a new Liberty.** Ludwig von Mises Institute, 2008.

[22] *Rothbard, Murray.* **Man, Economy & State.** Ludwig von Mises Institute, 2001.

[23] *Rothbard, Murray.* **Power & Market.** Ludwig von Mises Institute, 2006.

[24] *Rothbard, Murray.* **The Anatomy of the State.** Ludwig von Mises Institute, 2009.

[25] *Rothbard, Murray.* **The Ethics of Liberty.** New York University Press, 1998.

[26] *Svetski, Aleks & Moss, Mark.* **The Uncommunist Manifesto.** 2022.

[27] *Taleb, Nassim Nicholas.* **Antifragile.** Penguin Books, 2013.

[28] *Taleb, Nassim Nicholas.* **The Black Swan.** Random House, 2010.

[29] *Von Mises, Ludwig.* **Human Action.** Yale University Press, 1949.

## Podcasts

[1] *Breedlove, Robert.* **The "What is Money?" Show.**

[2] *McCormack, Peter.* **What Bitcoin Did.**

[3] *Snider, Jeffrey.* **Eurodollar University.**

www.ingramcontent.com/pod-product-compliance
Lightning Source LLC
Chambersburg PA
CBHW070613220526
45467CB00003B/1406